A GUIDE TO

WATTS GALLERY ARTISTS' VILLAGE

Published by Watts Gallery Trust
Watts Gallery
Down Lane
Compton
Guildford
Surrey GU3 1DQ

ISBN 978-0-9933902-0-3

With grateful thanks to the following who have helped enormously:
Ann Ayerst for photography **www.annayerst.com**
Anne Purkiss for photography **www.purkiss-images.eu**
Paul Taplin for photography **www.paultaplinphotography.com**
Chris Burchill for providing details on woodland birds
Fiona Curtis for providing the Compton Village Walk
Lorimer Burn for the aerial photography
Jane Turner for her advice

Map and bird illustrations by Donna Scott **www.donnascott.co.uk**
Design by Becky Hampson **www.beckyhampson.co.uk**

Front cover: Watts Gallery exterior and lawn © Watts Gallery
Back cover: GF Watts seated in his studio

All historical black and white photographs are from Watts Gallery, unless otherwise specified

ACKNOWLEDGEMENTS

Watts Gallery Trust is deeply grateful to the following for their generous support:

Patron HRH The Prince of Wales
Arts Patron Sir Antony Gormley OBE RA

Art Fund
Arts Council England
Clore Duffield Foundation
Country Houses Foundation
David Pike
The de Laszlo Foundation
The Deborah Loeb Brice Foundation
Esmée Fairbairn Foundation
The Finnis Scott Foundation
The Foyle Foundation
Garfield Weston Foundation
George and Kirsty Anson
The George John and Sheilah Livanos Charitable Trust
Guildford Borough Council
Heritage Lottery Fund
The Ingram Trust
The Isabel Goldsmith Patiño Foundation
J Paul Getty Jnr Charitable Trust
James and Clare Kirkman
Jonathan and Jane Clarke
The Linbury Trust
Matthew and Helen Bowcock
Nevill Keating Pictures
Peter Harrison Foundation
Professor Rob Dickins CBE
Richard Ormond CBE
The Sackler Trust
Sir Siegmund Warburg's Voluntary Settlement
Surrey County Council
The Wolfson Foundation

And all others who have so generously donated or given their support in different ways.

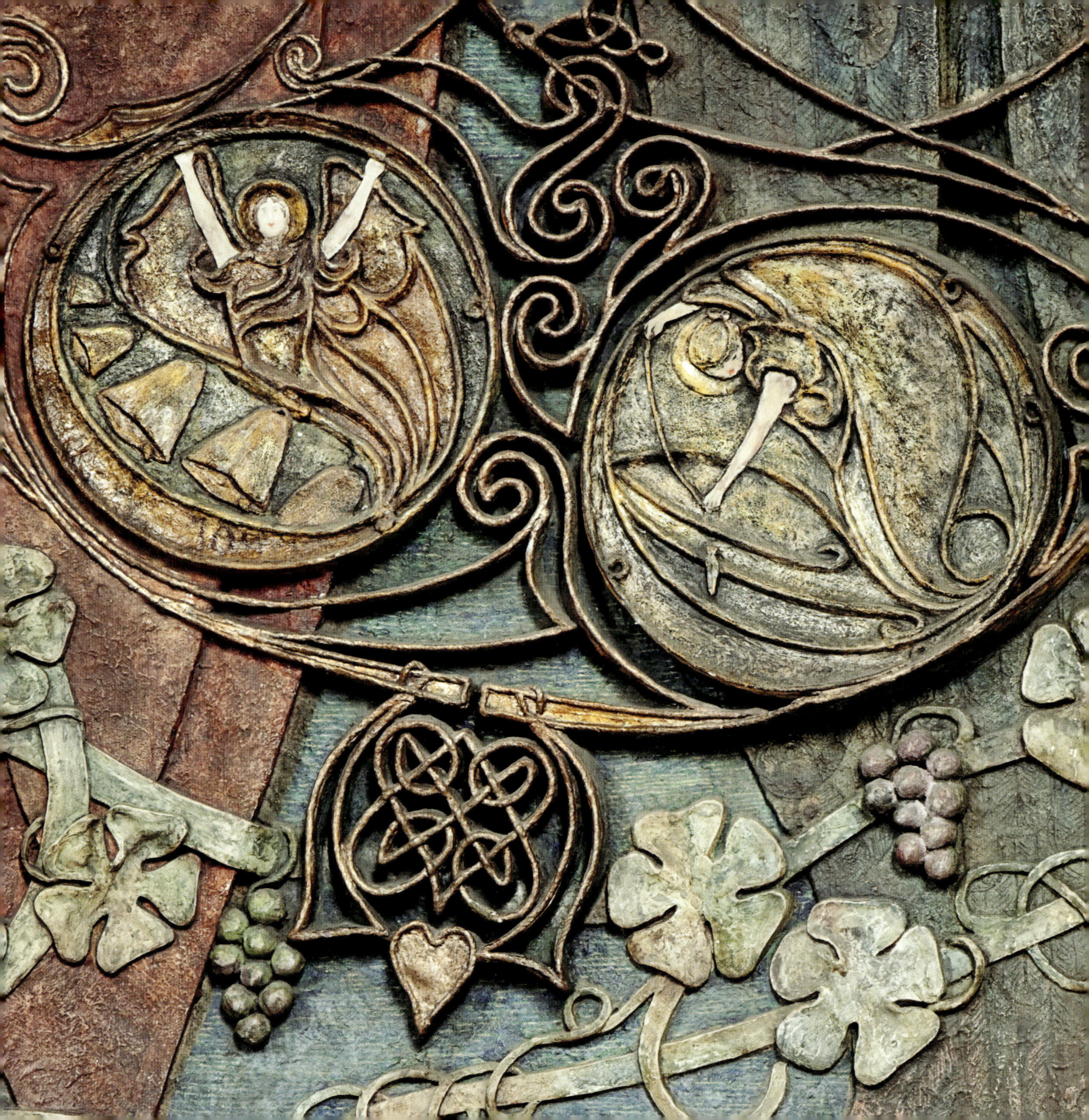

CONTENTS

LEFT
Angel medallions inside the Watts Chapel

DIRECTOR'S FOREWORD

Welcome to Compton. I hope that, like me, you will find that you always remember your first visit. A friend invited me to visit the Watts Chapel at the end of a long hot August day in 1990. As the shadows lengthened under the overarching beech tree, my children ran up and down the cobbled paths and we experienced the surprise of entering the highly ornate, rich red terracotta chapel. I thought how quintessentially English this placed seemed – a combination of ambitious ideas, mixed influences, social beneficence, visionary founders and a deep appreciation of nature and art – all hidden in a leafy hollow of the Surrey Hills.

I arrived at the hidden world of Watts Gallery as Director on 19 April 2004, Primrose Day, the anniversary of the death of Disraeli, another great Victorian. I explored one of the coldest places on earth, and was given the second telephone ever to be introduced into the gallery as well as the first ever computer. It has been a journey of discovery, ambition, courage and awe.

Richard Jefferies, the then Curator, was patient and welcoming and continued to play his piano in the Gallery on his day off on Thursdays. When it rained we all got wet. A stroke of luck was that Griff Rhys Jones decided to include Watts Gallery as one of the BBC *Restoration Village* wrecks in 2006 and the rest, as they say, is history. Dame Liz Forgan, then Chairman of the Heritage Lottery Fund, visited the Gallery and quietly said, as she looked at the holes in the roof, "you just have to go through the hoops".

I will never forget the day of 26 May 2011 when over 200 people crammed into the Gallery and gardens to shake the hands of TRH The Prince of Wales and the Duchess of Cornwall at the opening of the restored Gallery. Some of the Trustees were still incredulous that this building was now warm, lit, glowing and the paintings were all restored. Sandi Toksvig came to open the new Tea Shop in 2012, and we launched the Watts Contemporary Programme in 2013. In 2014 Simon Thurley of English Heritage came to preside at the handing over of the Watts Chapel to Watts Gallery Trust. And now, we begin the re-opening of Limnerslease. The Wattses' artists' village is coming back to life.

None of this would have been possible without the tireless and ceaseless help of those who live in Compton, those who have given their time and money, volunteers and staff who have given everything and those who have encouraged us on our path. Thank you!

Perdita Hunt OBE DL
Director, Watts Gallery – Artists' Village

TIMELINE

1817	George Frederic Watts born in London
1820s	Watts joins the studio of the sculptor William Behnes
1830s	Watts studies at the Royal Academy Schools
1843	Watts wins a major prize in the competition to decorate the new Houses of Parliament
1843–47	Watts lives and studies in Italy
1849	Mary Fraser Tytler born in India; she is raised in Scotland
1850s	Watts works on ambitious large-scale fresco projects
1864	Watts marries the actress Ellen Terry: they separate the same year
1870s	Mary Fraser Tytler studies art in London and meets Watts
1880–85	Retrospective exhibitions of Watts's work in Manchester, London and New York
1886	GF Watts and Mary Fraser Tytler married at Epsom in Surrey
1891	Mr and Mrs Watts take possession of their newly-built house, Limnerslease, at Compton
1895	Watts Chapel begun; Mary Watts begins her craft classes for local Compton people
1898	Watts Chapel consecrated; Mary Watts and her collaborators begin an expanded pottery enterprise, the Compton Potters' Arts Guild
1902	Watts admitted to the Order of Merit by King Edward VII
1904	Completion of the Watts Chapel decoration, opening of the Watts Gallery and death of GF Watts
1938	Death of Mary Watts and sale of the contents of Limnerslease
1940s	During the war years, Limnerslease used by Ardente, a company producing naval radar and sonar equipment
1952	Sale of Limnerslease
1956	Final closure of Compton Pottery
1959	Wilfrid Blunt becomes Curator of Watts Gallery
2011	Watts Gallery reopens after major restoration
2014	Watts Chapel and Cemetery come under management of Watts Gallery Trust
2016	Watts Studios at Limnerslease open to the public

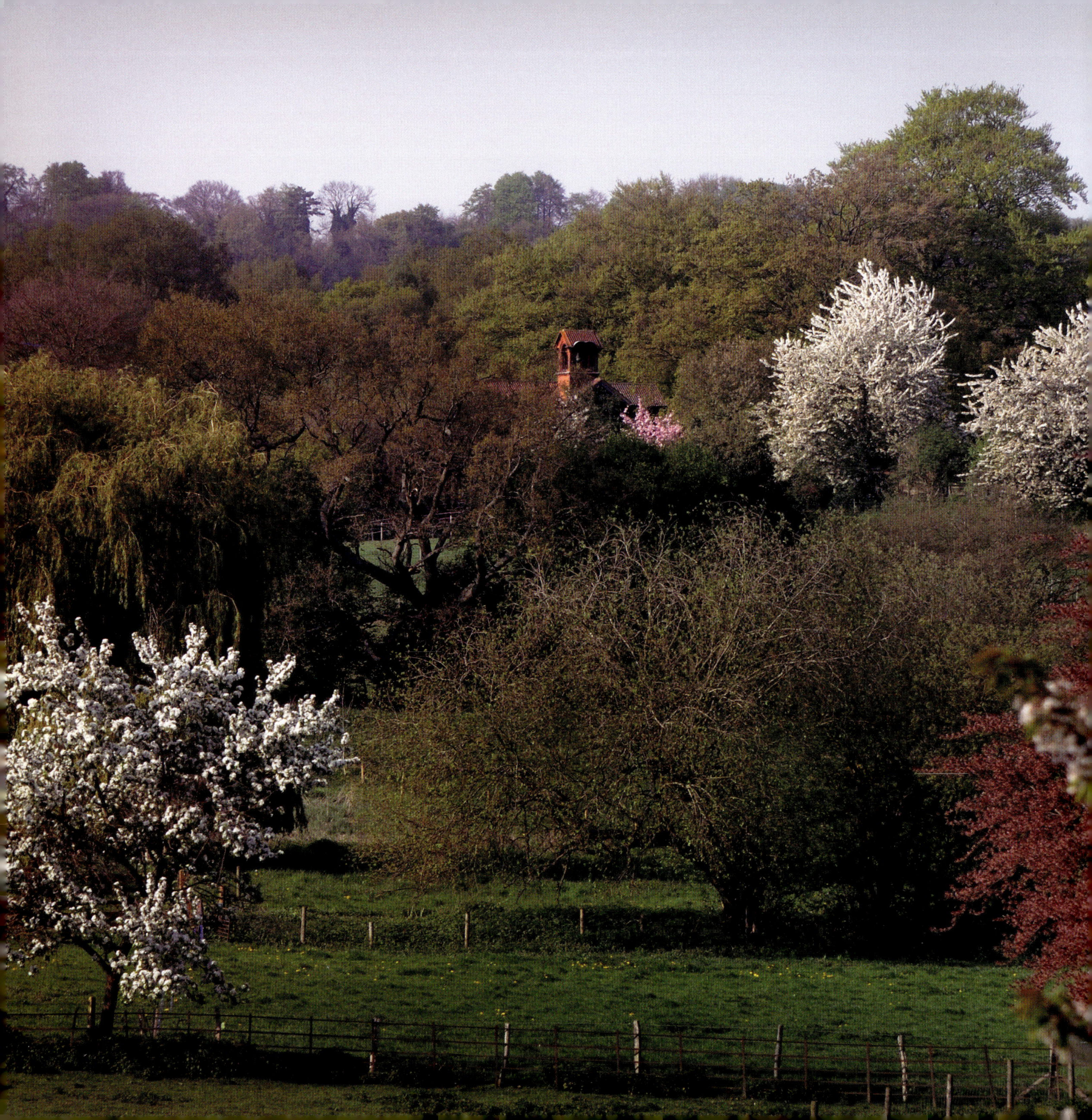

IN THE 1890s, TWO ARTISTS, GEORGE FREDERIC WATTS AND MARY WATTS, CREATED A UNIQUE GROUP OF BUILDINGS IN THE SURREY HILLS. AT COMPTON, NEAR GUILDFORD, THEY BUILT A HOUSE AND STUDIOS, A CHAPEL, POTTERY AND PICTURE GALLERY. THE ESTATE FLOURISHES AGAIN TODAY AS A LIVELY ARTISTS' VILLAGE.

LEFT
The Watts Chapel belfry visible across the fields

ARTISTS' VILLAGE

The artist George Frederic Watts (1817–1904) married the designer Mary Seton Fraser Tytler (1849–1938) in 1886. He was 69 and recognised as one of the greatest painters and sculptors of modern times; she was 36, an artist still seeking to find expression for her remarkable talents. Despite the difference in age, background and professional standing, the marriage was to be an especially happy one. Watts had always needed strong and talented women to support his art and fragile health, while Mary was looking for a noble cause to inspire her own creative powers. Their marriage allowed each to complete their hopes and dreams, and led to the creation of the Artists' Village at Compton.

G F Watts had been working for many years to develop a range of imagery that would express the fundamental truths of humanity. Compositions such as *Hope, Love and Life* and *Mammon* were seen by the late Victorians as the definitive icons of their age. Watts was more than a painter to his contemporaries: he was a visionary and a prophet.

One of the qualities which endeared Watts to so many was his readiness to help aspiring younger artists, to whom his high-minded themes of life, death and the progress of humanity offered a liberating alternative to the standard commercial products of the Victorian art world. Mary Fraser Tytler, from a Scottish gentry family, became one of these youthful acolytes of *Signor*, as his friends called Watts on account of his seniority and resemblance to a great master of the Italian Renaissance (although after their marriage Mary often referred to her husband rather less deferentially as her Little Lamb or Old Darling).

BELOW LEFT
GF Watts sitting next to the Della Robbia tondo at Limnerslease, c.1900

BELOW RIGHT
Watts Gallery sign; Benches in the grounds of the Artists' Village

RIGHT
Self-Portrait of GF Watts in Old Age, 1903–04

FAR RIGHT
GF Watts, *Mrs GF Watts*, 1887

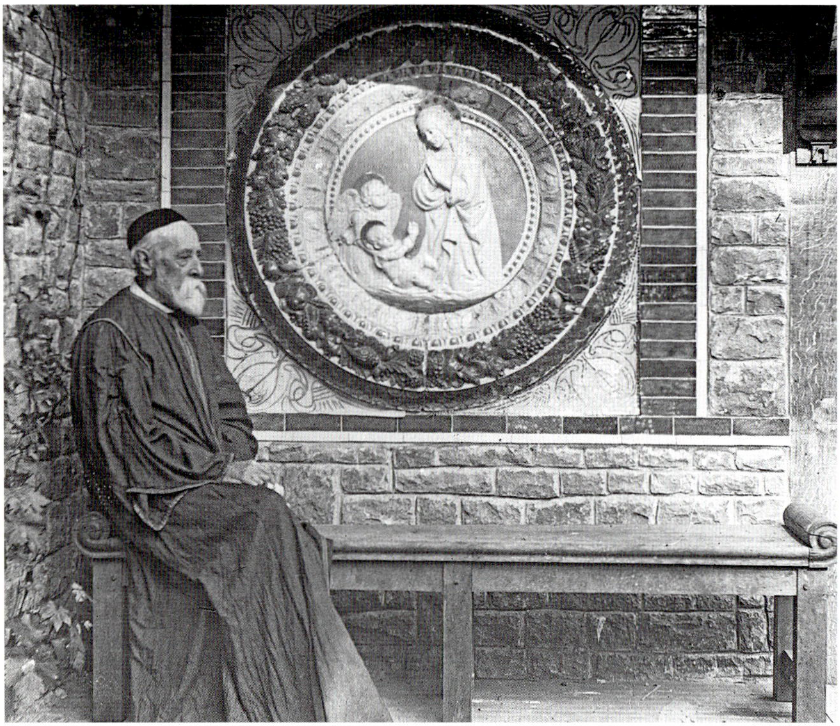

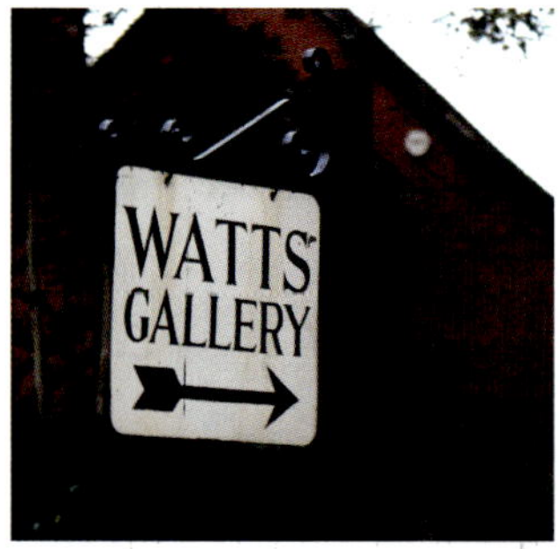

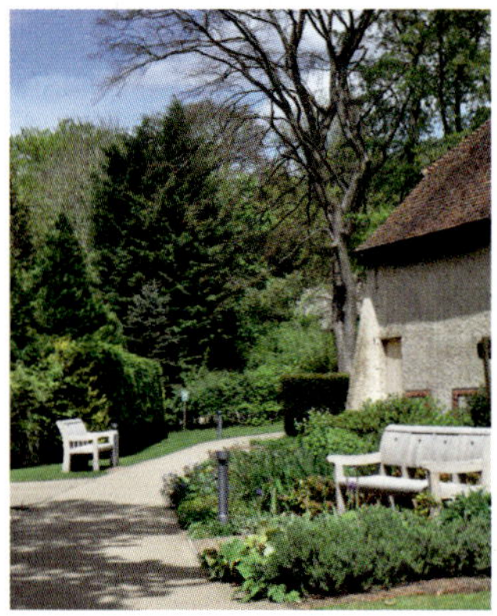

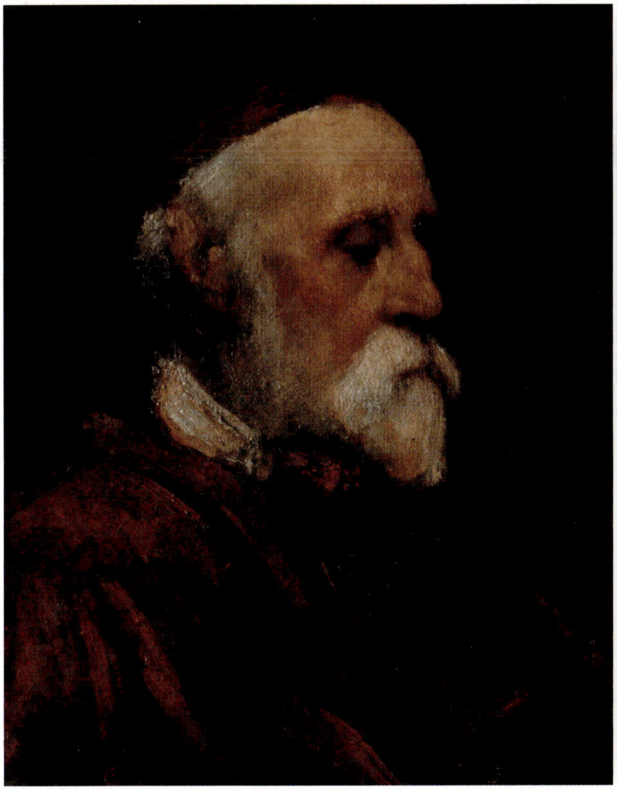

IT WAS NOT TILL 1870 THAT I FIRST WENT UNDER ITS THATCHED PORCH, AND WAITED IN THE ROOM OF THE BLUE CEILING TILL SUMMONED TO THE STUDIO, TO PASS WITH A BEATING HEART THROUGH A RED BAIZE-COVERED DOOR. THERE WE READ WITH SOME FEELING OF AWE A LARGE LABEL – "I MUST BEG NOT TO BE DISTURBED TILL AFTER TWO O'CLOCK" – BEFORE IT WAS PUSHED BACK, TO SWING AGAIN HEAVILY BEHIND US; THE STUDIO DOOR OPENED, AND SIGNOR CAME FORWARD TO MEET US ... FROM THIS TIME FORWARD I RECEIVED THE GREATEST KINDNESS AND HELP FROM HIM. HIS PATIENCE WITH AMATEUR WORK, HIS APPRECIATION OF ANYTHING THAT WAS A NATURAL EXPRESSION IN ANY ART, IS SO WELL KNOWN THAT NOTHING FURTHER NEED BE SAID.

Mary Watts recalling her first meeting with Watts, at Little Holland House, where he lived in London; from *Annals of an Artist's Life*, 1912

The Wattses' honeymoon took them to Egypt, Istanbul and Athens. Having determined to focus upon design work (leaving painting to her husband), Mary was immediately inspired by the range of different cultures she encountered, each with their own traditions of myth and symbolism but which seemed to her to form a kind of common visual language.

Wishing to secure a winter residence as a regular bolthole from London, the Wattses settled on Compton near Guildford in Surrey. They moved into Limnerslease, the house they built at Compton, in 1891. They were able to enjoy it for only thirteen years until Watts's death in 1904, but they made the most of those years, spending more and more time there.

Samuel Barnett, who ran philanthropic and artistic projects in London's East End in which both Watts and Mary had been involved, visited them in 1896 and reported:

> *Yesterday we went to stay with Mr and Mrs Watts at their country house near Guildford. We found them established on a hillside amid the fir trees with peeps toward Hindhead. Their house just teems with art and ideas. The ceiling is worked in plaster, each panel symbolical of some religion – the walls varied with oak and drapery, pictures, chairs, everything is suggestive. He and she were, as ever, humble, inspired, devoted.*

Once mistress of her own home, there was no stopping the newly confident Mary's ambitions as a designer. She began with the extraordinary ceiling decorations at Limnerslease noted by Samuel Barnett, and by 1895 was teaching local people how to work in clay. Together with her Compton collaborators, Mary built the Watts Chapel and created its stunning decoration. On the back of the skills and experience developed through this project, she established a pottery business which became the Compton Potters' Arts Guild.

By the turn of the century the pottery had its own building across

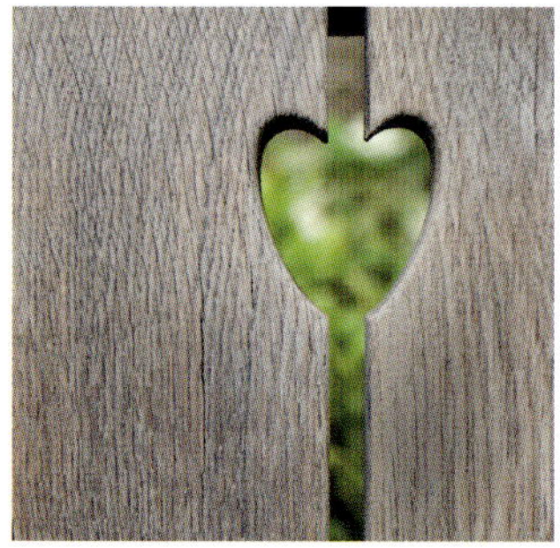

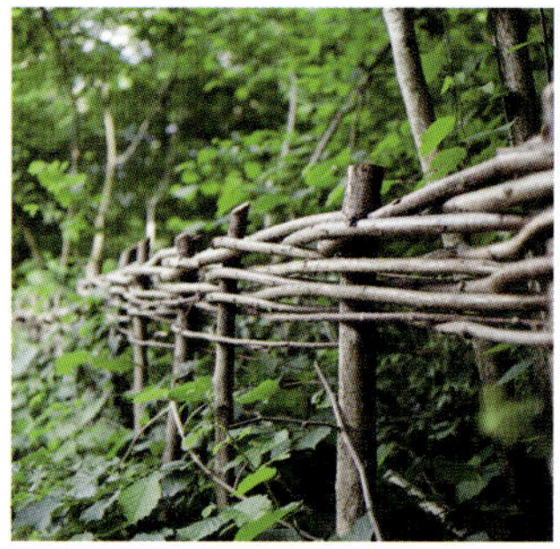

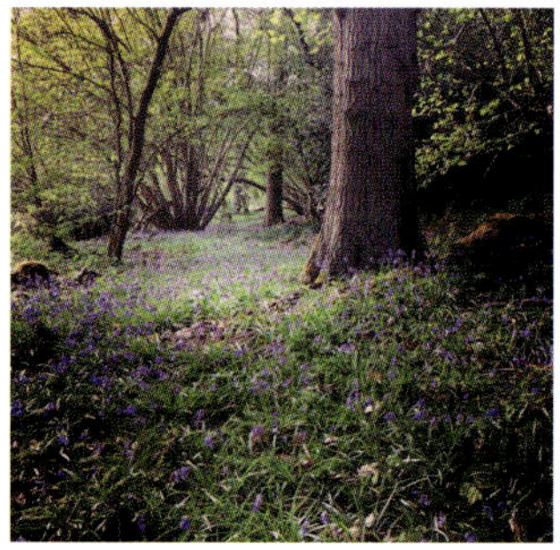

ABOVE (TOP – BOTTOM)
Bench in the Gallery grounds; Willow fence; Bluebells in the woodland

RIGHT
Watts Gallery lawn

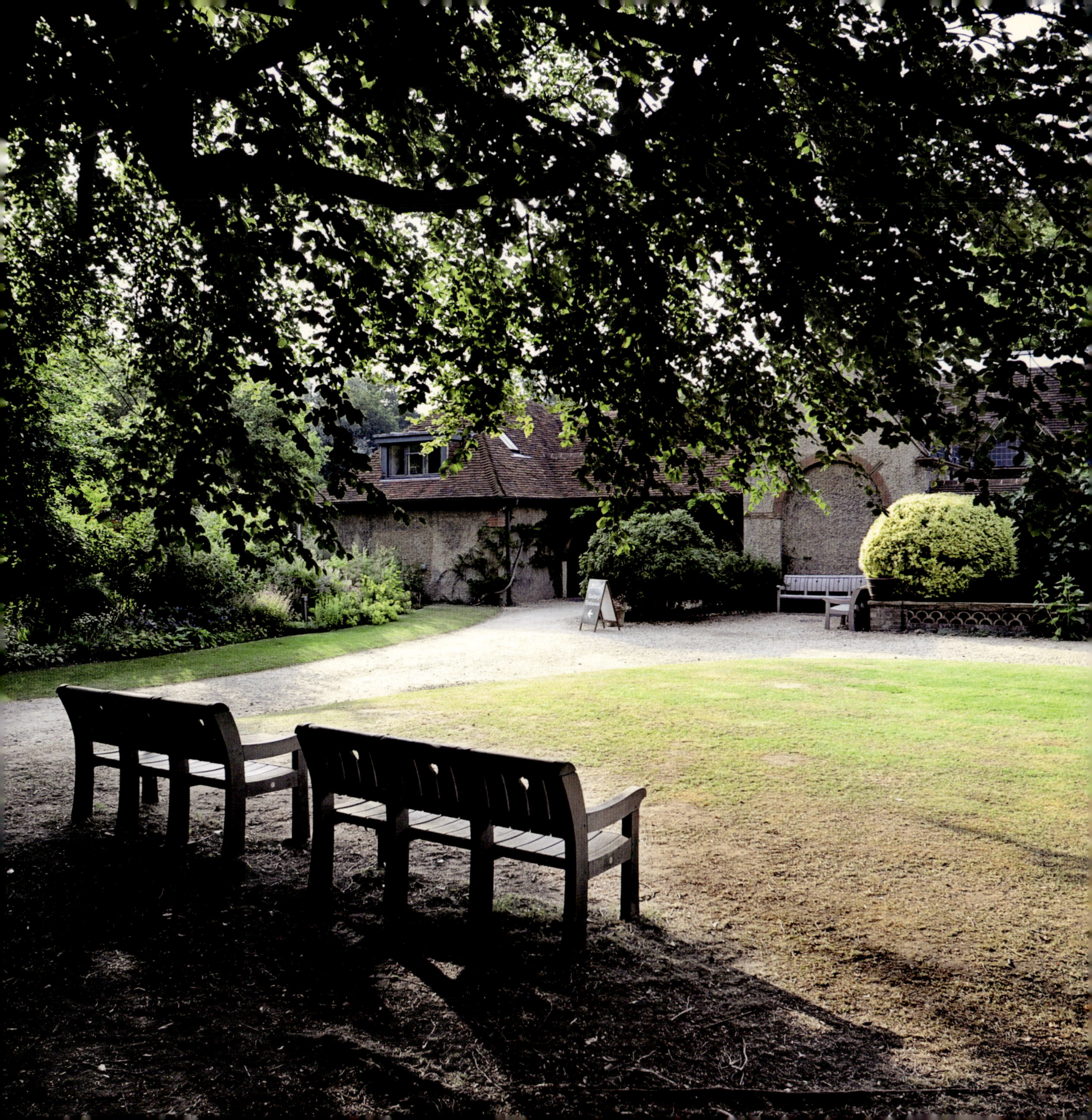

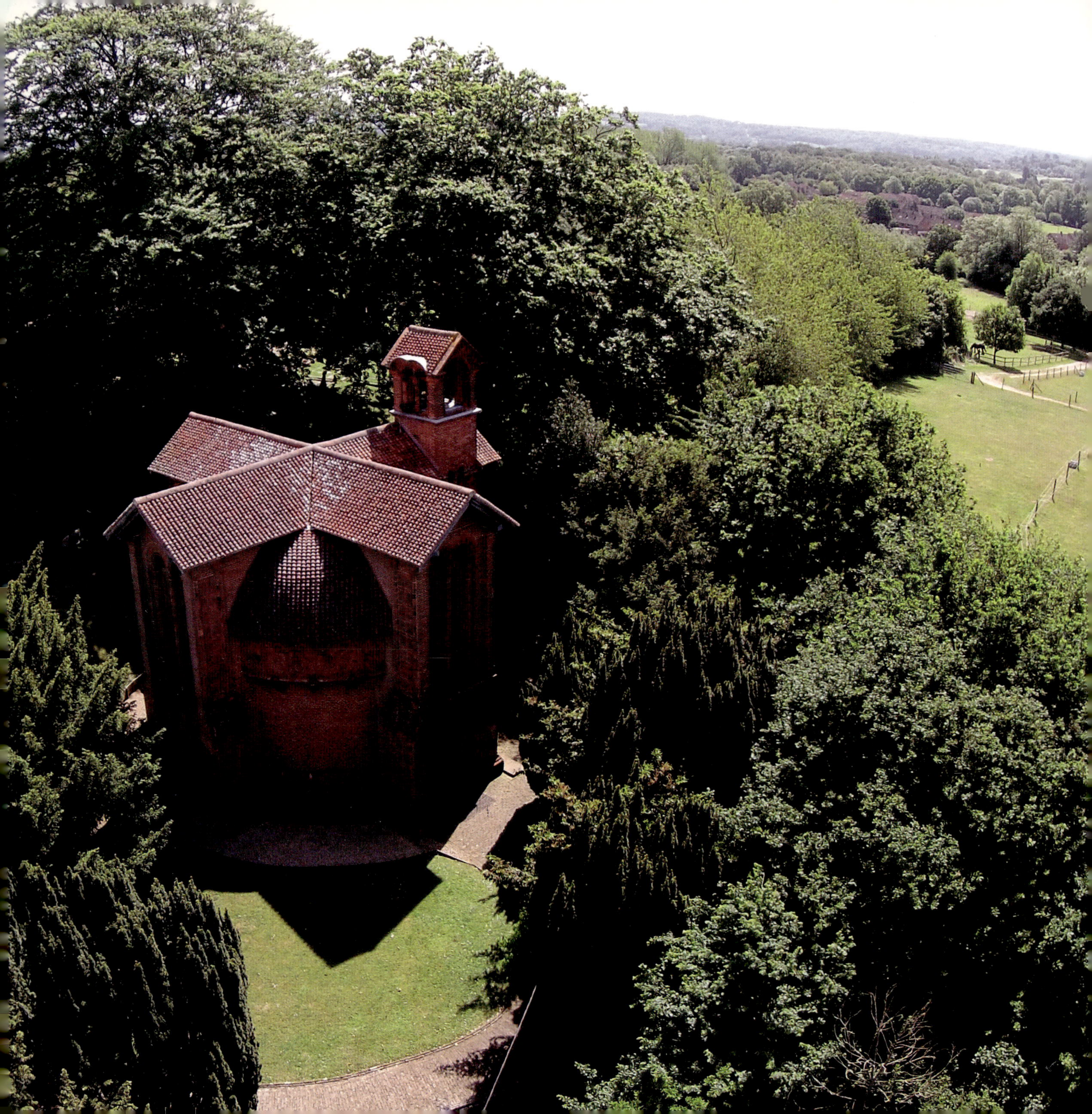

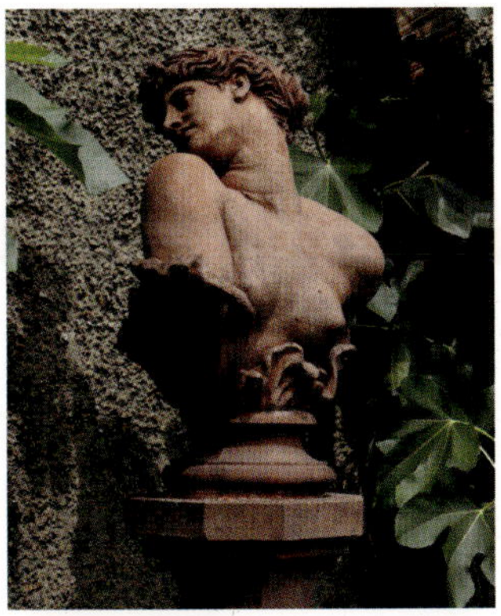

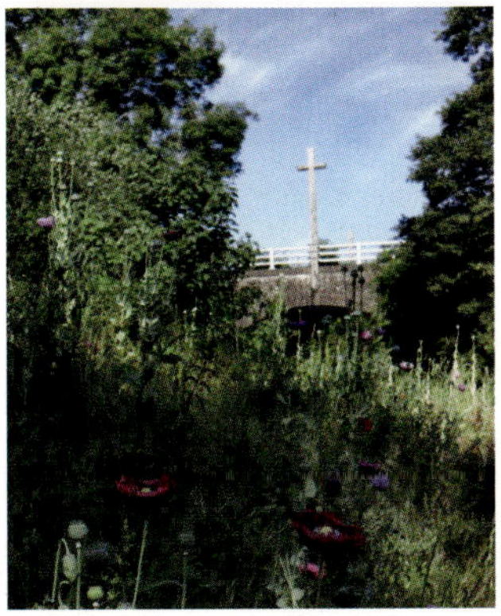

LEFT
Aerial view of the Watts Chapel

ABOVE (TOP)
Terracotta bust of *Clytie*

ABOVE (BOTTOM)
View of the Lutyens bridge over the Pilgrims' Way, near Limnerslease

Down Lane from Limnerslease, and this in turn led to the building of what became Watts Gallery, opened in 1904. The Watts Gallery, a charismatic Arts and Crafts building, was, perhaps uniquely in the history of art and architecture of this period, both a hostel and a picture gallery. Its prime function was to provide accommodation for the apprentices at the pottery, but it also incorporated carefully designed rooms in which to display the works of Watts.

GF Watts died on 1 July 1904, having lived just long enough to see both the completed Watts Chapel and the opening of the Watts Gallery. Soon afterwards Mary sold their London house and settled permanently at Limnerslease. She was joined by Lilian Macintosh, who had first come to live with the Wattses as an orphaned teenager in 1898 and became their ward.

Mary died in 1938 and the pottery closed in the 1950s. Limnerslease was sold and divided into different properties. The Watts Artists' Village shrank to the Watts Gallery which managed to survive – just – the twentieth century, during most of which Victorian art was sadly undervalued.

In recent years, an ambitious campaign to restore the Gallery has been undertaken, one consequence of which was the realisation of how much of the rest of the original Artists' Village remained, ready to be reborn. With the leasing to the Watts Gallery Trust of the Watts Chapel and Cemetery in 2014, and the opening of the Watts Studios at Limnerslease in 2016, the Watts Artists' Village has indeed come back to life. Once again Compton "teems with art and ideas", inspired by GF and Mary Watts and committed, as they were, to contributing Art for All to the modern world.

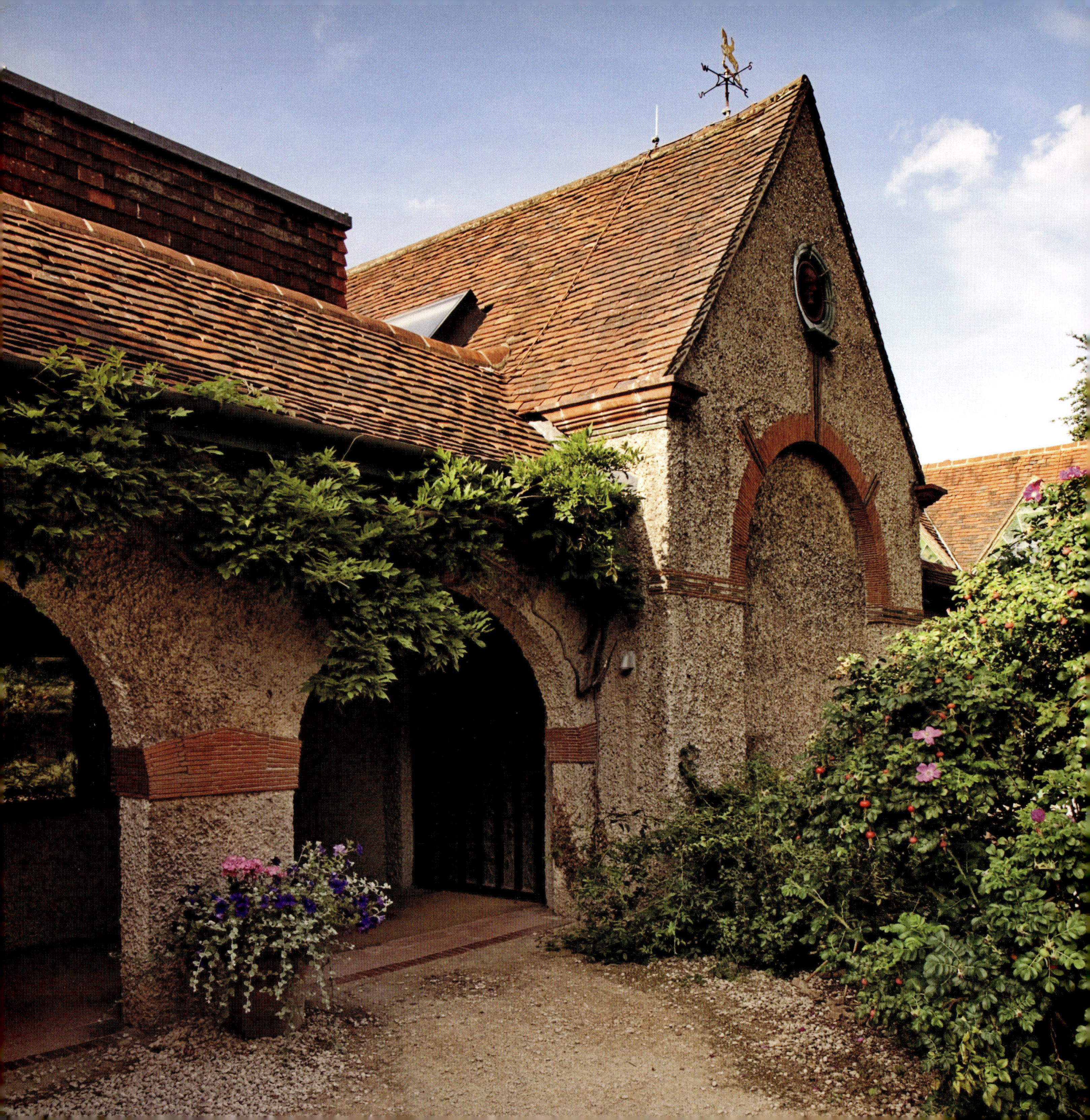

THE ART OF GF WATTS OFFERS US VISIONS OF THE HUMAN FORM IN TRANSFORMATION. INSPIRED BY THE MAJESTY OF GREEK AND RENAISSANCE ART, WATTS CREATED SUBLIME IMAGES WHICH SPOKE POWERFULLY TO HIS VICTORIAN CONTEMPORARIES. THE MOST EXTENSIVE COLLECTION OF HIS WORK IS HELD HERE AT COMPTON.

LEFT
Watts Gallery entrance

GF WATTS AND THE WATTS GALLERY

George Frederic Watts (1817–1904) was one of the great artists of the nineteenth century. As a young man he exhibited alongside Turner and other famous Romantic painters at the Royal Academy, and by the end of his life he was a crucial influence upon the young Picasso. A retiring, philosophical man, Watts was at the same time intimate with many of the famous and influential figures of the Victorian age – he could count Gladstone and Tennyson among his friends and his first wife was Ellen Terry, the leading actress of the period.

Watts was recognised by his contemporaries as something much more than a painter of pictures. Watts's imagery offered the Victorians – and later, the wider world – a vision of nothing less than the progress of the human soul in an age of materialism and spiritual doubt.

Watts felt himself outside the mainstream of modern British art, and to belong rather to a noble tradition of sculptors and painters who addressed the great themes of life, love and death, narrating these timeless subjects through representations of the human body. Watts painted some wonderful landscapes, but throughout his very long career it is consistently the human form that is at the centre of his work. Watts's painted bodies are striking for their sculptural form – his training as a sculptor is clear even in his paintings, in which the artist made sure never to lose sight of his outlines.

This way of approaching the human form also helped make Watts the greatest of Victorian portraitists. His sitters seem solidly present, on account of Watts's sculptural understanding of form, and yet, in his best portraits, there is at the same time a strong sense of the mind at work separately from the body. In his portraits Watts succeeded in showing the spirit working through the body just as he did in his larger allegorical or symbolist works.

I PAINT IDEAS, NOT THINGS. I PAINT PRIMARILY BECAUSE I HAVE SOMETHING TO SAY, AND SINCE THE GIFT OF ELOQUENT LANGUAGE HAS BEEN DENIED ME, I USE PAINTING. MY INTENTION IS NOT SO MUCH TO PAINT PICTURES WHICH SHALL PLEASE THE EYE, AS TO SUGGEST GREAT THOUGHTS WHICH SHALL SPEAK TO THE IMAGINATION AND TO THE HEART AND AROUSE ALL THAT IS BEST AND NOBLEST IN HUMANITY.

GF Watts

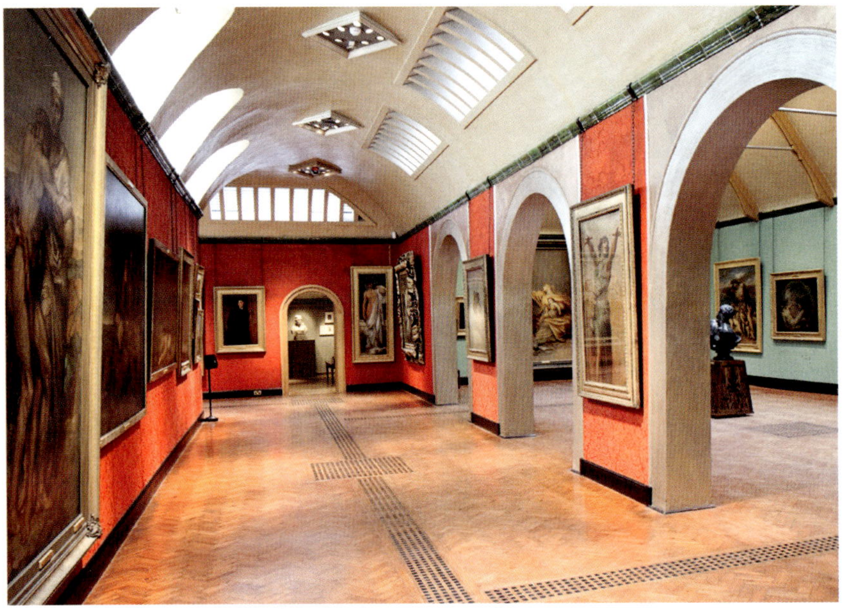

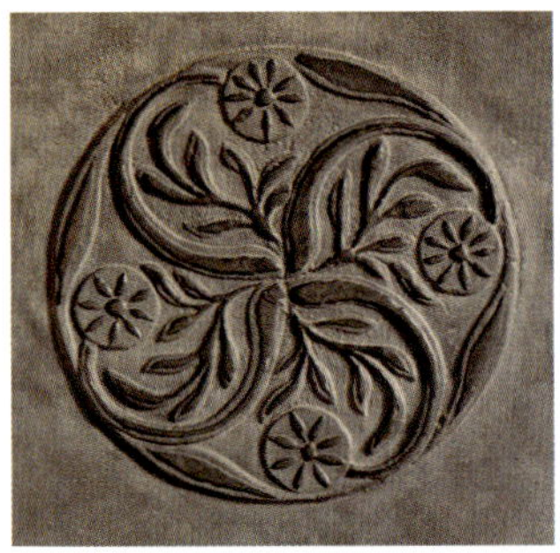

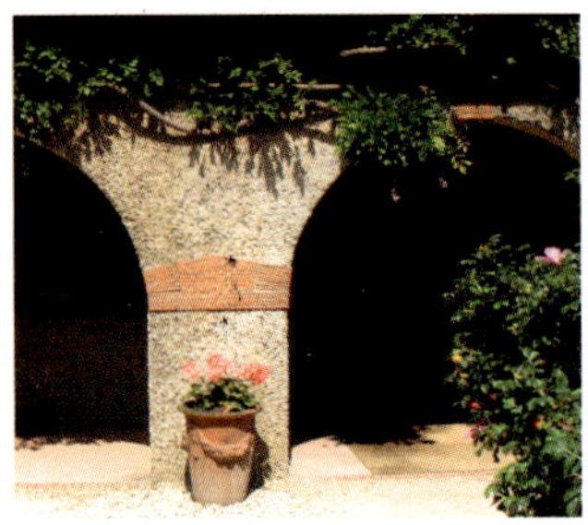

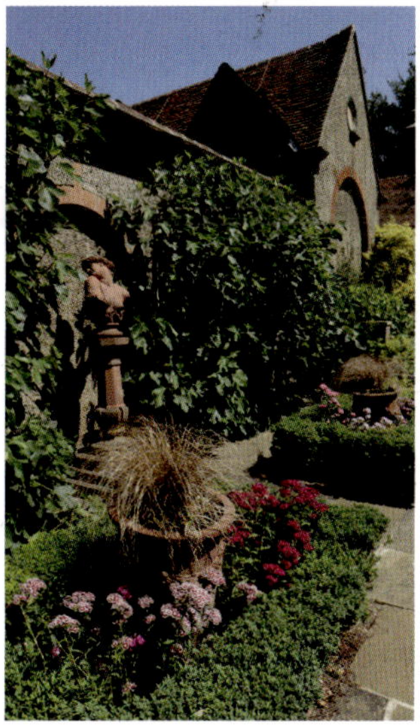

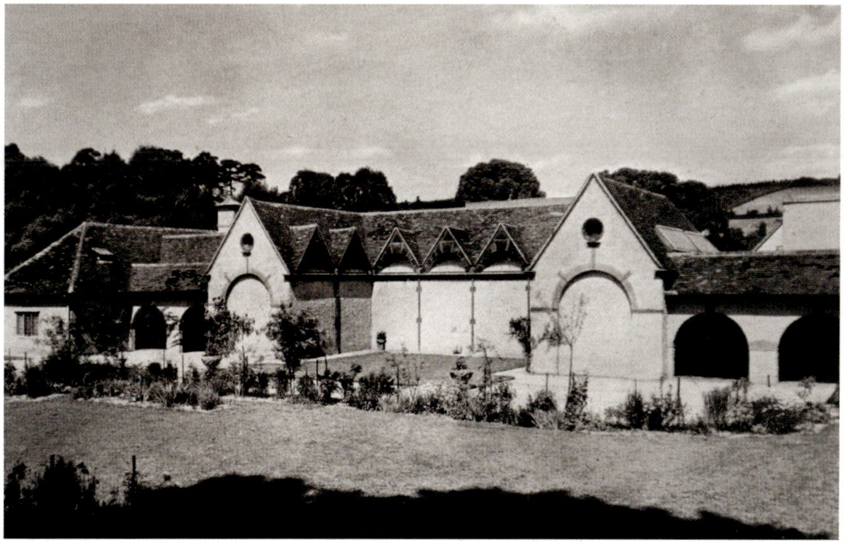

FAR LEFT
The Weston Gallery

LEFT (TOP)
Detail of a motif on one of the Gallery's lead doors

LEFT (BOTTOM)
Watts Gallery's Loggia

ABOVE LEFT
Watts Gallery sunken courtyard

ABOVE RIGHT
Watts Gallery exterior, c.1904

Over many years Watts built up a collection of portraits of his great contemporaries which he donated to the National Portrait Gallery. Known collectively as the Hall of Fame, this series includes famous Victorians such as William Morris and John Stuart Mill. Only one woman was included, however: Josephine Butler, the fearless social reformer, who Watts painted at Limnerslease in 1895.

From the 1870s Watts had his own studio-house in Kensington, to which he added a picture gallery open to the public on weekend afternoons. After the Wattses acquired a second home, Limnerslease, in Compton in the 1891, they built another picture gallery here: the Watts Gallery. This extraordinary building was designed by a local architect, Christopher Hatton Turnor, in an Arts & Crafts style. Turnor recalled that "dear old Signor" had asked him to build a picture gallery but "to keep it a simple and rural type of building". It combines local materials, such as the ceramic tiles, on a rendered concrete structure. Originally the building was intended also as a hostel for the male apprentices in the pottery, housed in the wings of the Gallery. It must have been a wonderful place to live whilst training as a craftsman. Today it is Britain's only purpose-built public museum devoted to the art of a single professional artist.

Watts lived just long enough to see the Gallery opened to the public on 1 April 1904, his paintings displayed against the rich red colour he always preferred, with simple labels written by the artist offering some hints towards the meanings of the pictures on display. After Watts' death the Gallery was soon extended, with a larger room added, painted in contrasting green, as well as a sculpture gallery.

Between 2006–11 Watts Gallery Trust worked with architects ZMMA to achieve the sensitive restoration needed to ensure the Gallery's survival for a further hundred years. The structure of the building was made sound, and thorough research was undertaken into the colours and fittings of the interior and into the ways in which the pictures had been hung in the past. The resulting building, modernised but returned to its original appearance, won admiration from both the public and specialist architectural critics.

The restored Gallery is now able to host an ambitious exhibitions programme. Subjects of recent exhibitions have included Russian Arts & Crafts, Richard Dadd and paintings and ceramics by Evelyn and William de Morgan. At its core remains the Gallery's unrivalled collection of some 250 paintings and 800 works on paper by Watts, displayed as the artist himself desired.

THE NOBLEST ART IS IN A GREAT DEGREE SYMBOLIC, DWELLING UPON THAT WHICH IS GENERIC AND GENERAL, MAKING USE OF THE SIMPLEST FORMS, OR RATHER EXTRACTING AND SELECTING THE SIMPLEST PROPERTIES FROM OUT OF THE RICH MASS OF INFINITE DETAIL, PRESENTING A GRAND WHOLE TO THE MIND RATHER THAN EXPLAINING THE WHOLE PIECEMEAL.

GF Watts

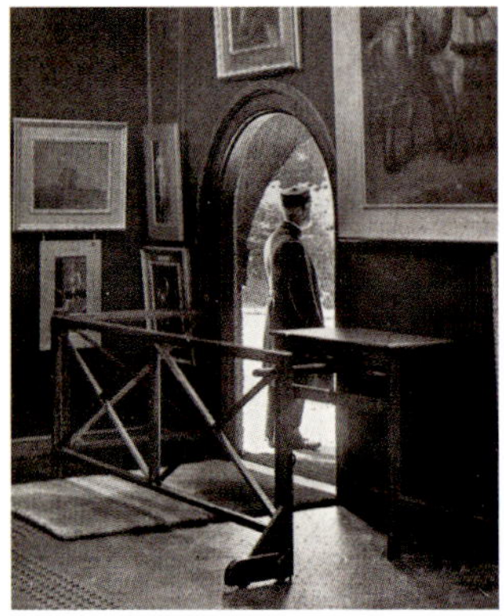

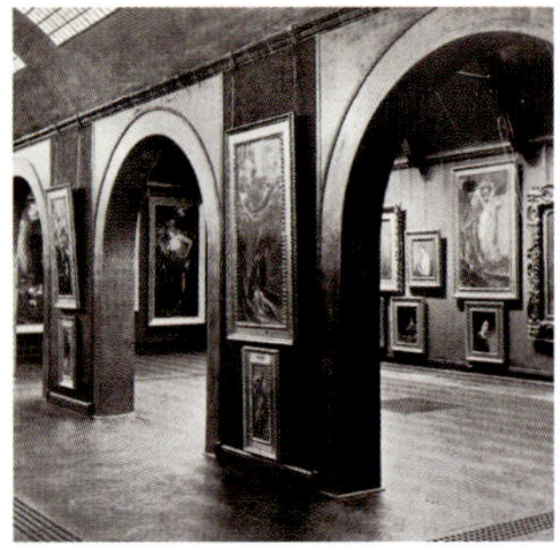

ABOVE (TOP)
Entrance to the Livanos Gallery, c.1904

ABOVE (BOTTOM)
Gallery interior, early 20th Century

HIGHLIGHTS FROM THE PAINTINGS COLLECTION

BELOW

Found Drowned | oil on canvas | c.1848/50

Returning to London from Italy, Watts undertook a series of confrontational paintings on the theme of the destitution he saw in the capital's streets. 'Found drowned' was the polite expression used to refer to someone who had committed suicide by throwing themselves into the Thames. A clue to this woman's tragedy must be contained in the locket in her cold hand.

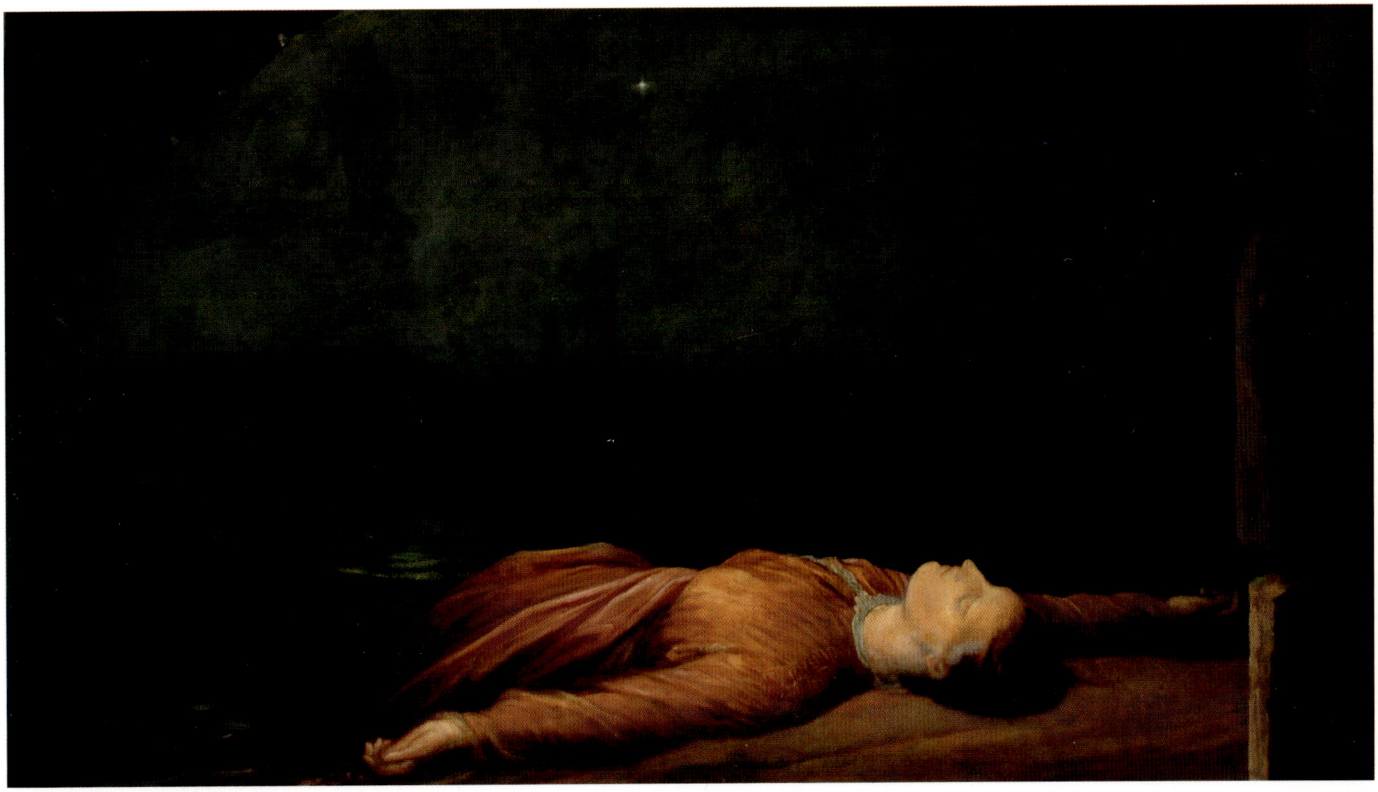

Adopted by David Pike

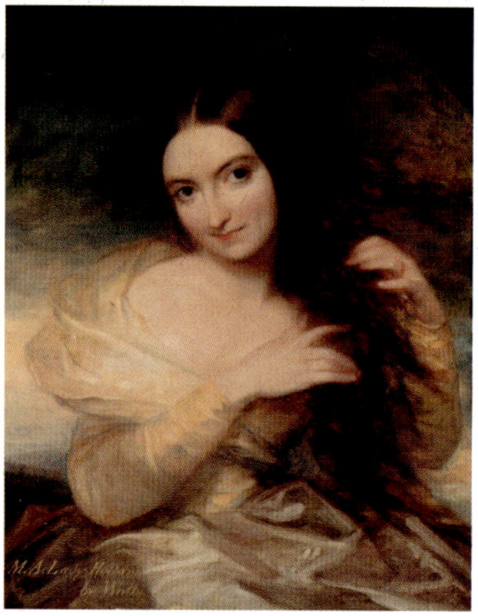

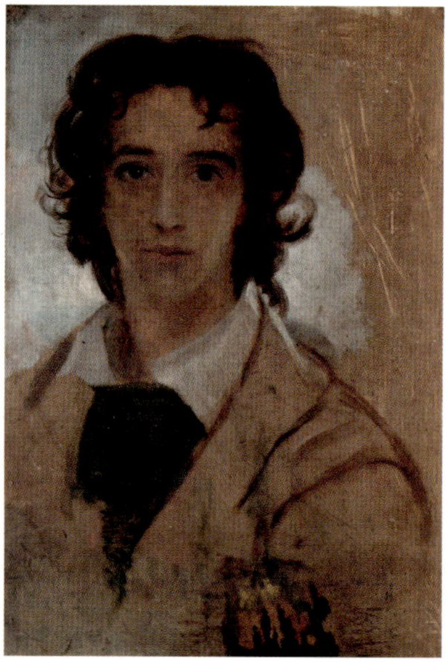

Adopted by Dr John & Sheila Dobson

LEFT (TOP)

Lady Holland | oil on canvas | c.1844

Watts spent several years studying in Italy during the 1840s. In Florence he was taken up by Lord Holland, a British diplomat. His wife, Mary Augusta, Lady Holland, was one of many aristocratic ladies upon whom Watts was to depend during his life. He shows her here in a very informal pose, caressing her undone hair.

LEFT (BOTTOM)

Portrait of the Painter at the Age of Seventeen | oil on canvas | 1834

Already a professional artist when he painted this self-portrait, the young Watts appears as the archetypal romantic young genius, looking longingly to the future.

OPPOSITE PAGE (LEFT)

Self-Portrait | oil on canvas | c.1853

Watts shows himself here at the age of about 36. He was at this point living in the grounds of Holland House in Kensington, the long-term guest of Sara Prinsep, a society hostess and supporter of the arts. Watts was able to focus on some very ambitious projects, painting huge pictures on the walls of public and private buildings. He is dressed in the style of a Renaissance intellectual, suggesting how completely he identified with his calling as an artist.

OPPOSITE PAGE (RIGHT)

Portrait of Virginia Dalrymple | oil on canvas | c.1871–74

Watts painted many portraits of close friends, not least members of the circles around Little Holland House, the house in Kensington where he lived for many years. The striking sitter here was the niece of his hostess Sara Prinsep.

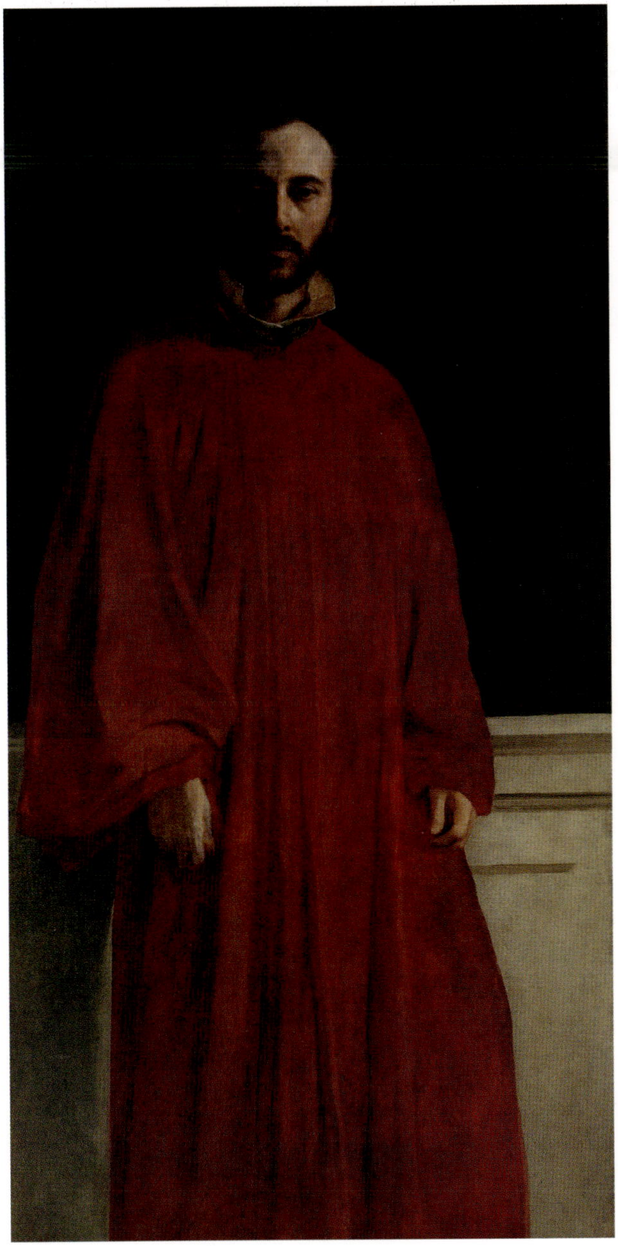

Acquired by Watts Gallery Trust with the help of The Heritage Lottery Fund, Art Fund, The V&A Purchase Grant Fund, Compton Village Association and Compton Parish Council

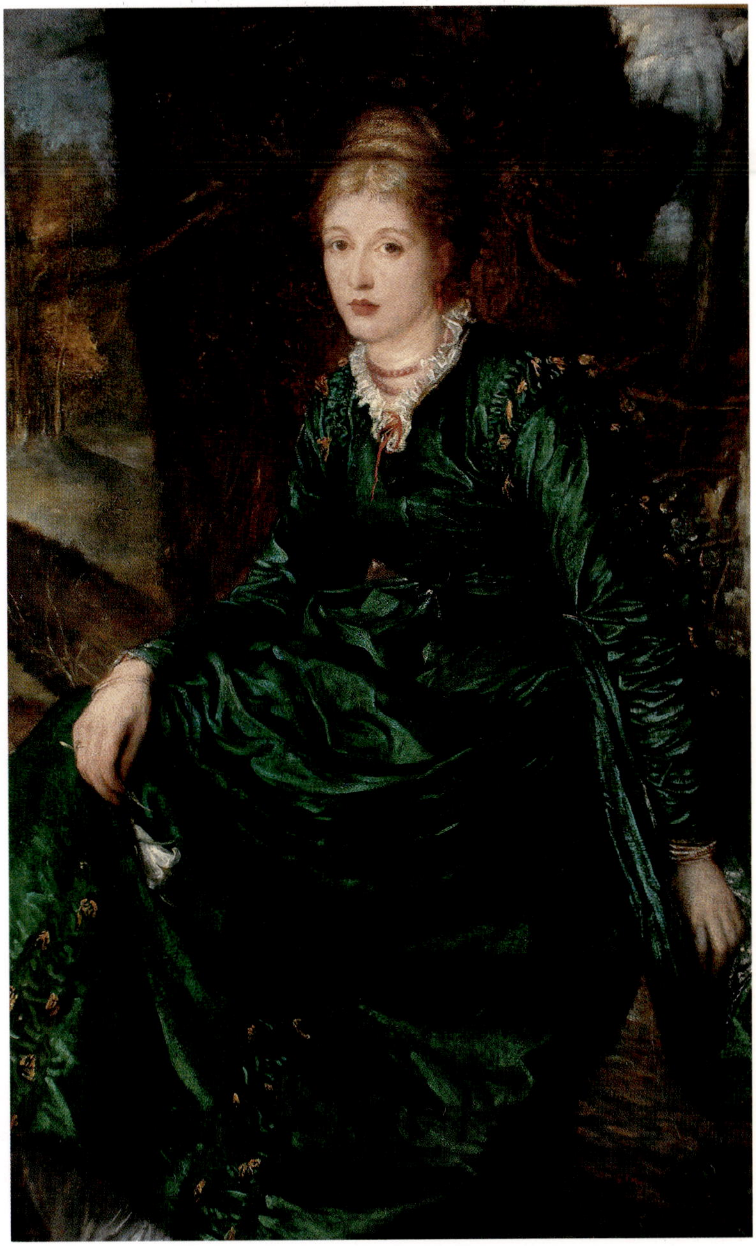

Adopted by Jane Knox

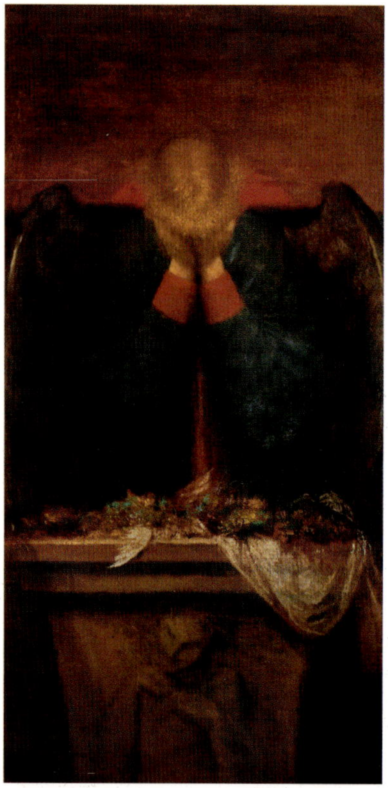

Adopted by HK Associates

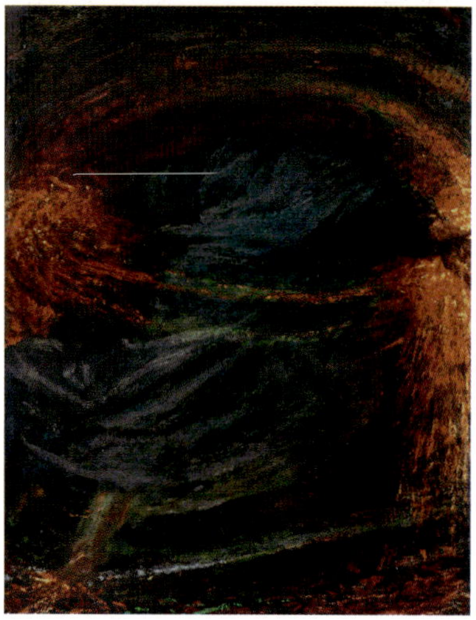

Adopted by Anthea Vernell

LEFT (TOP)

A Dedication | oil on canvas | 1898–99

This painting's full title is *A Dedication to all those who love the beautiful and mourn over the senseless and cruel destruction of bird life and beauty.* Watts was passionately fond of birds and could not bear the use of their feathers to ornament women's hats. An angel is shown mourning the remains of birds sacrificed to fashion on the altar of vanity. The angel was modelled by Lilian Macintosh (later Chapman) who came to live with the Wattses as their ward in 1898.

LEFT (BOTTOM)

The Sower of the Systems | oil on canvas | c.1902

One of the artist's last compositions, this bold painting is nothing less than the elderly Watts's effort to find an image of the Creator with which to replace the 'kind, white-bearded old man' which he had long rejected. A faceless figure scatters light into the darkness, sowing the beginnings of the universe. It is an attempt to personify the unified laws of science. At the end of his career, Watts's belief in the power of art to embody the highest truths had not diminished.

OPPOSITE PAGE

Paolo and Francesca | oil on canvas | c.1872–84

The adulterous lovers from Dante's *Divine Comedy* are being blown around by a never-ending wind in a circle of hell. Watts became fascinated with the subject whilst travelling in Italy in the 1840s. The deep folds in the drapery, the reflections of light and the sallow skin give the figures a monumental, sculptural presence. Watts often held onto his works until he was completely satisfied: *Paolo and Francesca* took over a decade to complete and was put on show in the gallery of his London house.

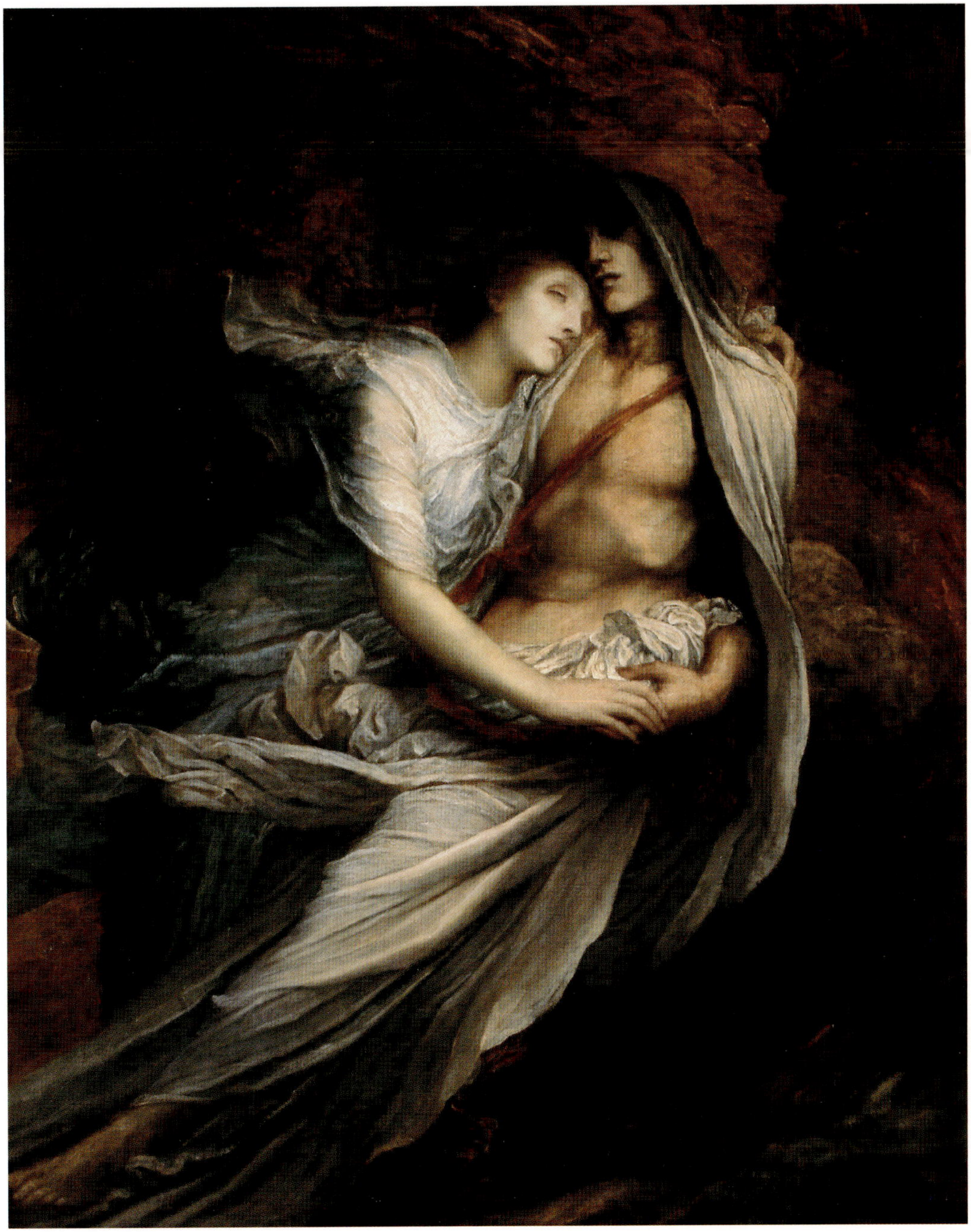

Adopted by Lady Verey

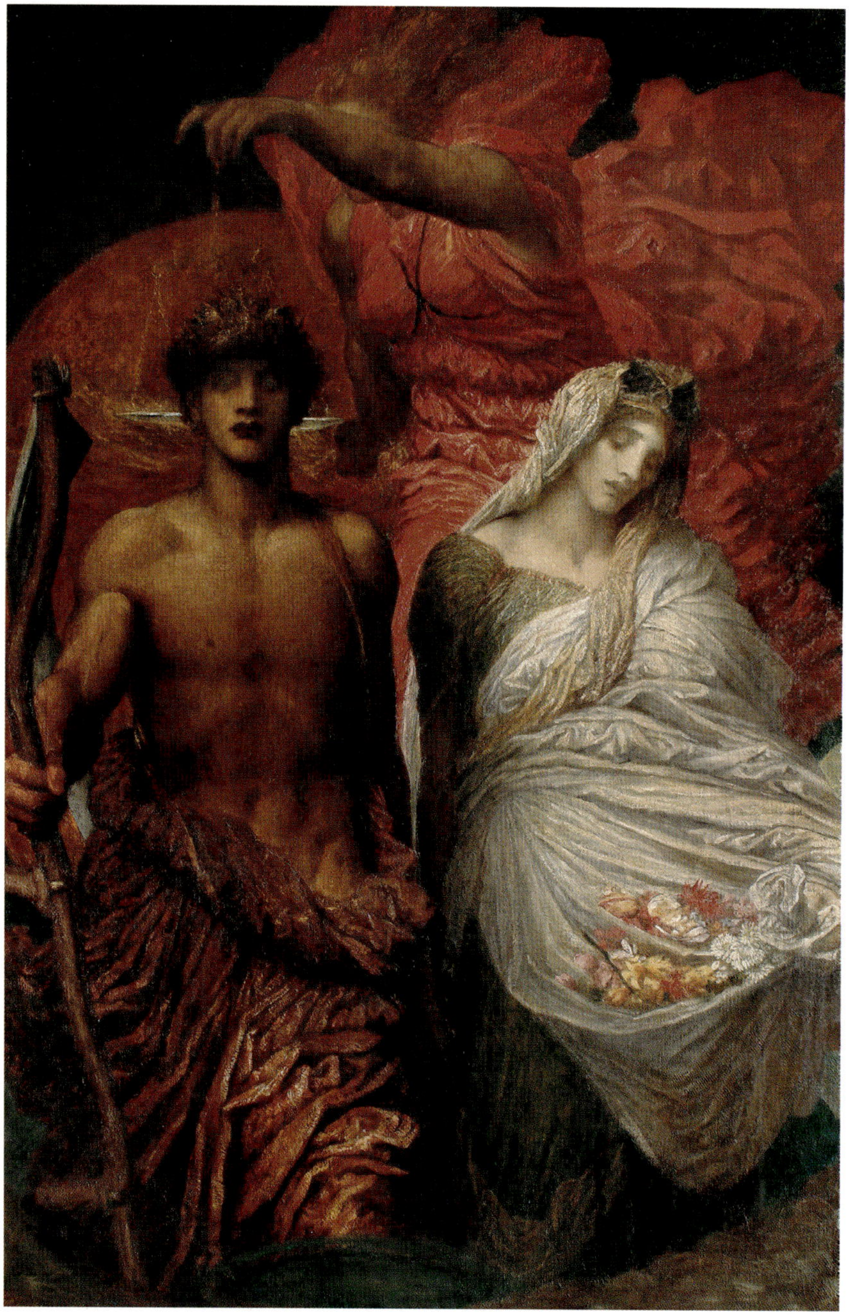

LEFT

Time, Death and Judgement
oil on canvas | late 1870s-1896
Watts often reversed traditional personifications when creating his ambitious allegorical works. Instead of a wise Old Father Time, here Watts gives us a cruel, blind athlete, striding unrelentingly forward. He is partnered by the figure of Death, a young and beautiful woman who gathers cut flowers. Justice rises in their wake – and seems to be seeking to halt the march of Time. This painting hung prominently in St Paul's Cathedral for most of the twentieth century.

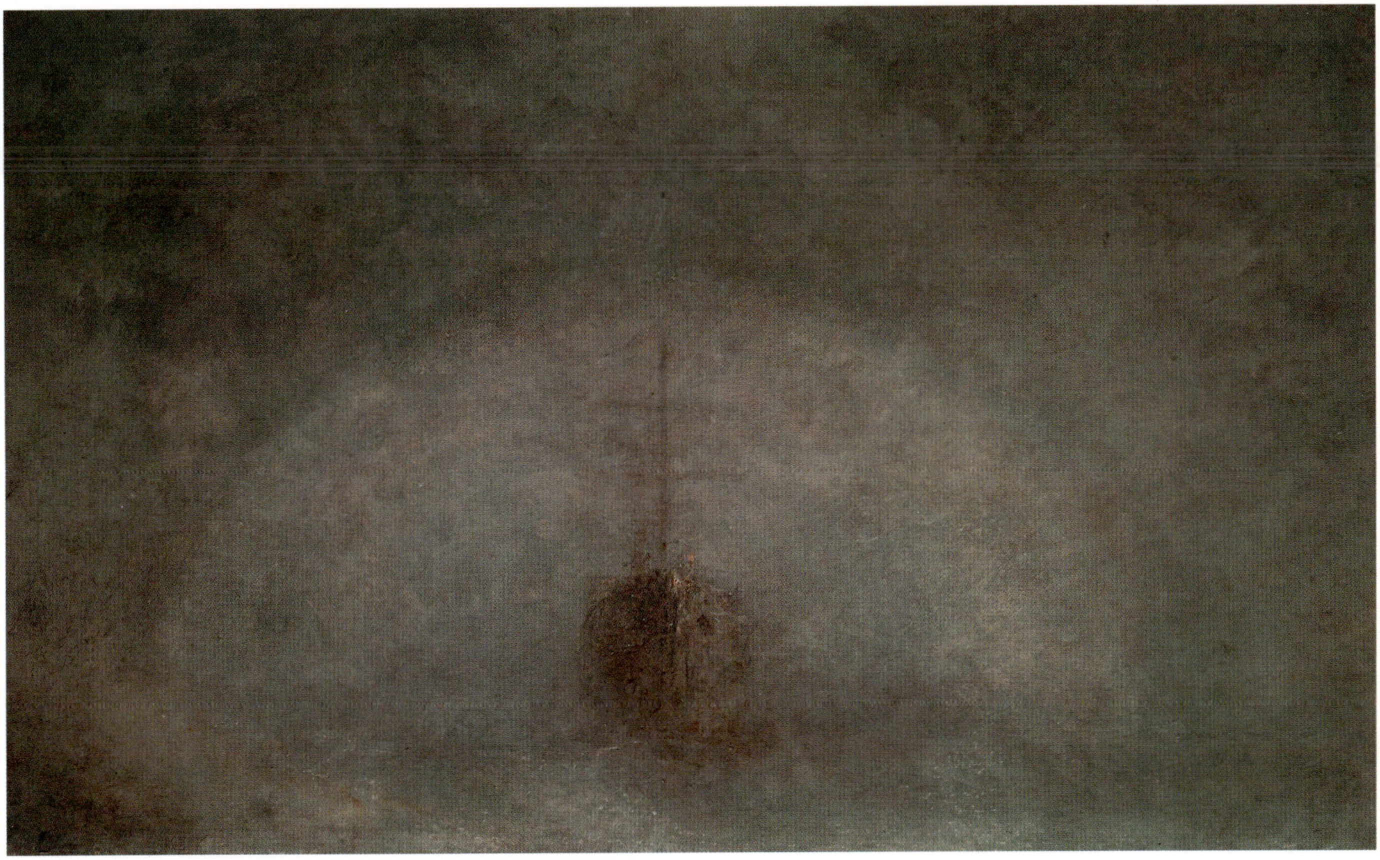

Adopted by Shalford Decorative and Fine Arts Society

ABOVE

A Sea Ghost | oil on canvas | 1887

Mary Watts records that during the Wattses' honeymoon in 1887 they were passengers on a boat off the Italian coast which was commandeered to tow another damaged vessel. Watts's haunting image of the towed ship, following him through an eerie sea mist, contains echoes of Turner, but is at the same time one of Watts's most Symbolist creations.

The Adopt a Watts scheme offers you the opportunity to have a personal association with an artwork in the collection ensuring its preservation and long term care. For more information please visit: **www.wattsgallery.org.uk/support-us/adopt-watts**.

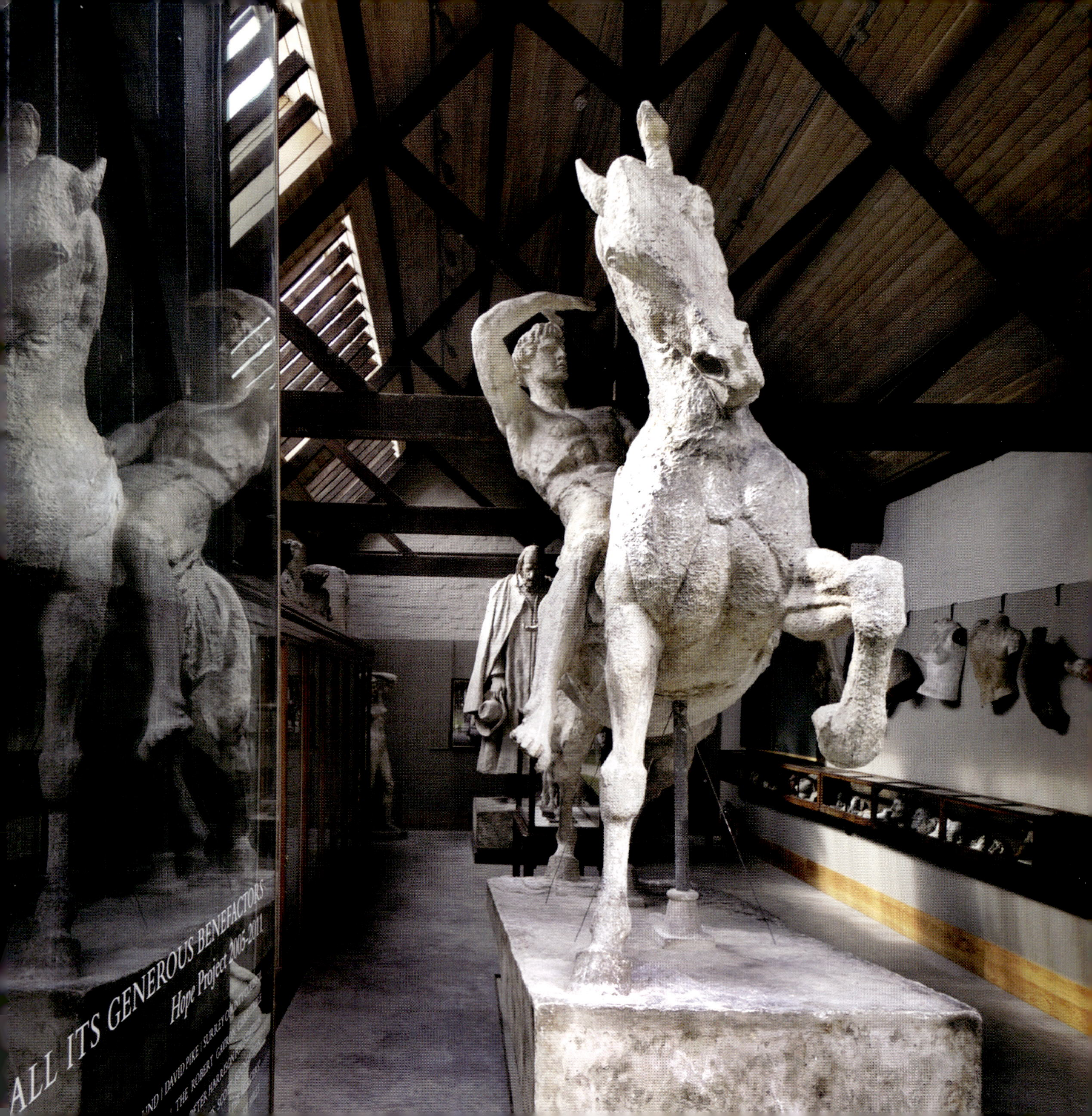
ALL ITS GENEROUS BENEFACTORS
Hope Project 2005–2011

THE SCULPTURE GALLERY HOUSES THE TWO MONUMENTAL WORKS WHICH WATTS COMPLETED AT THE END OF HIS LIFE, 'PHYSICAL ENERGY' AND 'TENNYSON'. DISPLAYED WITH THEM ARE THE THREE-DIMENSIONAL MODELS, SKETCHES AND PORTRAITS WHICH WATTS MADE USE OF WHEN DEVELOPING HIS EPIC SCULPTURES.

LEFT
G F Watts, Full-scale gesso model for *Physical Energy*, 1884–1904
Adopted by John Lewis OBE

SCULPTURE GALLERY

Aged only ten, Watts joined the Soho studio of the sculptor William Behnes, where he was able to study drawing as well as observe the techniques of modelling, carving and casting that allowed images to be created in three dimensions.

A few years later Watts began a lifelong study of the works which he acknowledged as his inspiration – the Ancient Greek sculptures from the Parthenon in Athens (the Elgin Marbles, in the British Museum) of which the artist later wrote: "The Elgin Marbles were my teachers. It was from them alone that I learned". The lessons Watts took from Greek sculpture – the melancholy grandeur, the sense of static power – were applied primarily to painting.

It was not until the 1860s that Watts had the confidence publicly to exhibit a sculpture. This was *Clytie*, shown at the Royal Academy in 1868. Clytie was a nymph who, hopelessly in love with the sun god Helios, strained

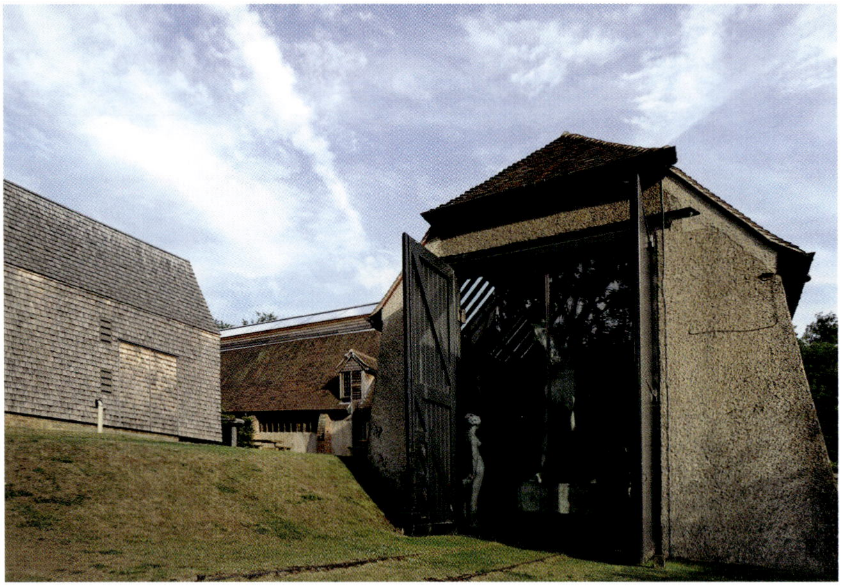

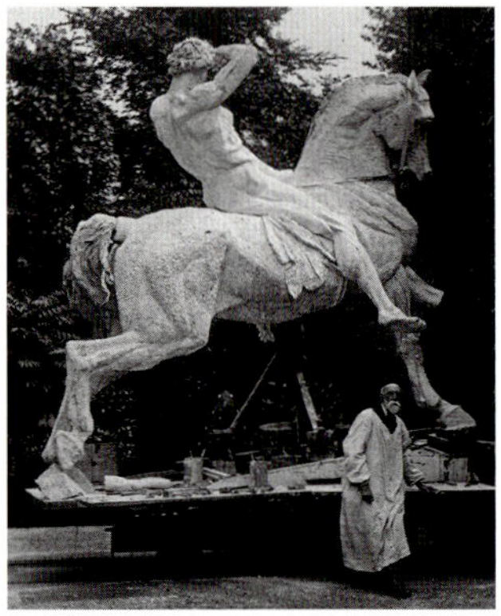

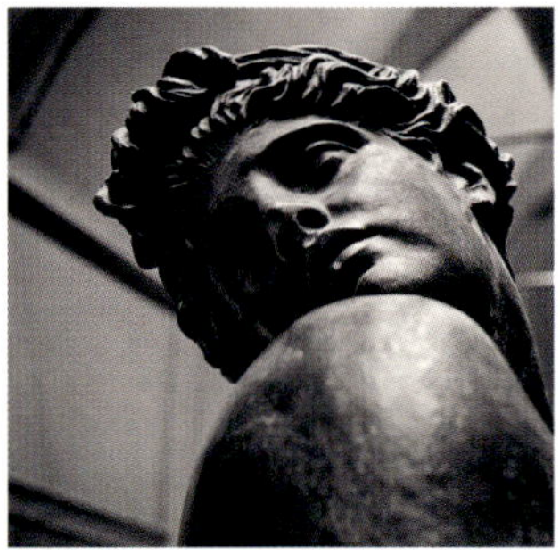

her neck to watch his transit every day. Watts was fascinated by the human neck throughout his career, and *Clytie*, of which the Gallery possesses a bronze cast, is his most powerful treatment of this theme.

The success of *Clytie* seems to have led to a series of monumental commissions commemorating deceased worthies. One of these commissions came from the Duke of Westminster who wanted a massive equestrian figure of his Norman ancestor Hugh Lupus, the first Earl of Chester. From this, Watts evolved another huge sculpture of a man on a horse, the work that became *Physical Energy*.

Intended to express a basic component of human nature – our bodily instinct to press forward, with or without reason – *Physical Energy* stands on the frontier of Modernist sculpture. On display is the original plaster model from which the final bronze casts were made. Mixing rag into the plaster (to create what was known as *gesso grosso*) allowed Watts to create something like a very soft stone into which he could carve.

ABOVE (LEFT)
The Sculpture Gallery showing *Physical Energy*

ABOVE (TOP)
Watts posing with the gesso model of *Physical Energy* in the garden of his London home

ABOVE (BOTTOM)
Bronze bust of *Clytie*

UNFAILINGLY, AFTER BREAKFAST THE GREAT HORSE AND ITS RIDER ROLLED OUT FROM THE SCULPTURE STUDIO INTO THE GARDEN, AND THE WORK ON "PHYSICAL ENERGY" WENT ON. UP ON LADDERS AND DOWN BELOW ON THE STAGE THE FIGURE IN THE WHITE SMOCK WORKED ON TIRELESSLY.

Mary Watts describing her husband at work in London in 1887; from *Annals of an Artist's Life*, 1912

Casts of *Physical Energy* were set up outside Cape Town in South Africa, as part of the memorial to the colonial statesman Cecil Rhodes, and in Kensington Gardens in London. The model, meanwhile, was returned to the artist who continued to develop it until his death in July 1904. It now dominates the Sculpture Gallery along with another huge plaster model – for the memorial to Watts's close friend, the great poet Alfred Tennyson.

The massive figure of Tennyson was commissioned by Lincoln Cathedral, and created by Watts at Limnerslease in an adapted barn near the entrance to the house's driveway. Watts gives his figure a sublime and contemplative stillness, having been inspired by Tennyson's poem to a *Flower in the Crannied Wall* which ends: "Little flower – but if I could understand / What you are, root and all, all in all, / I should know what God and man is."

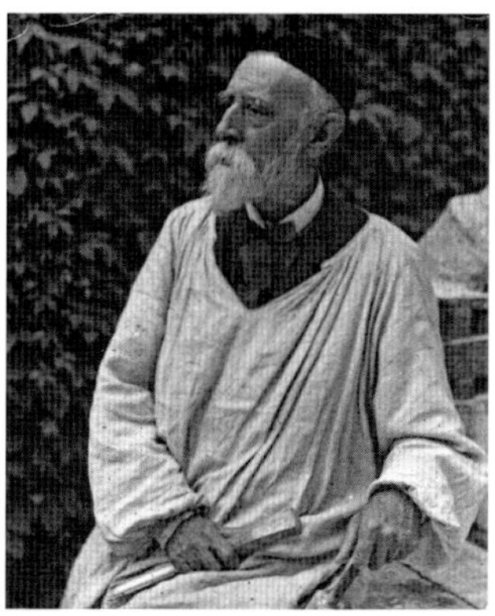

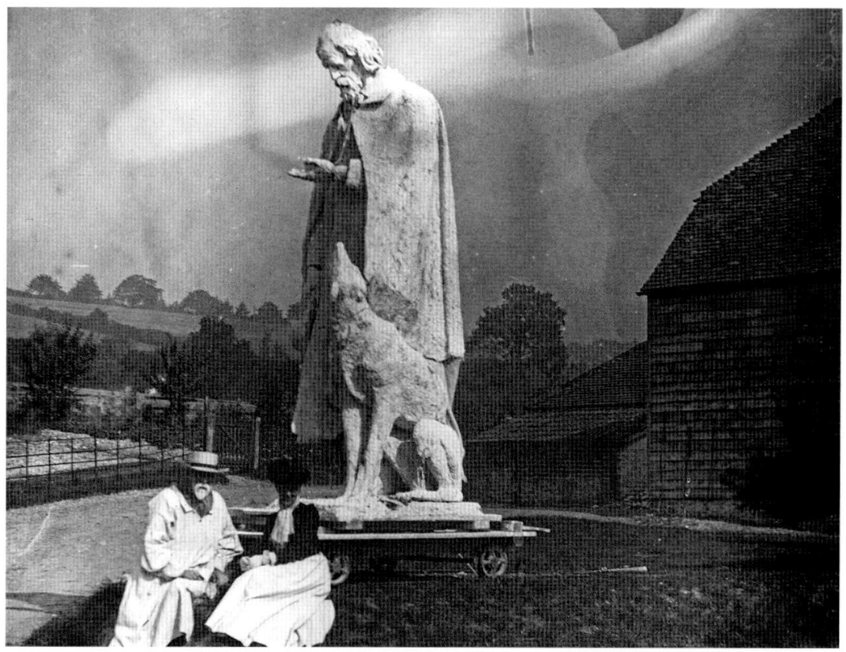

ABOVE AND RIGHT
GF Watts with his sculpting tools; GF and Mary Watts sitting outside the barn studio, in the grounds of Limnerslease, with the *Tennyson* sculpture behind, c.1899

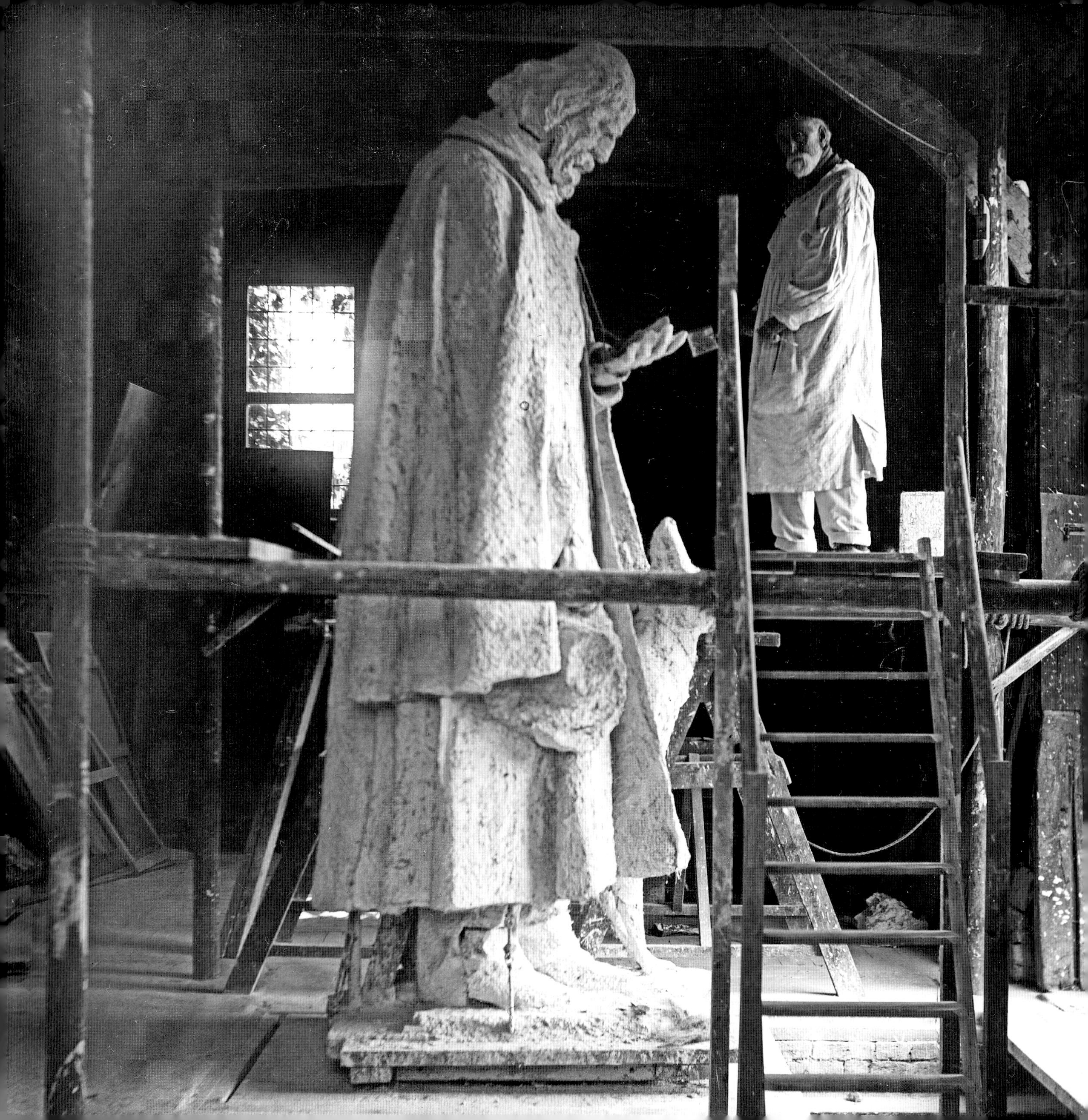

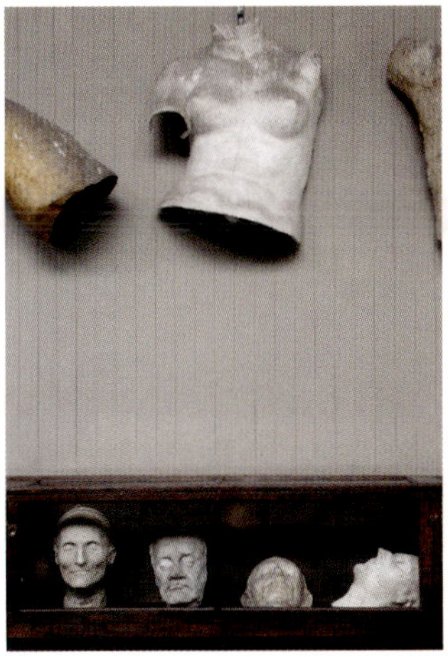

In the Sculpture Gallery the visitor can also see some of the many ways in which Watts painstakingly built up his compositions using sculptural fragments of the body. Scarcely using live models, Watts often preferred to copy from plaster casts of arms, heads, legs – even ears. Mary Watts records her husband making a model from his own body, "studying from his own finely wrought leg".

In addition to many anatomical and art-historical sculptural fragments, Watts owned a small collection of death masks – plaster casts of faces taken immediately after death – as well as portrait busts of people, both historical and contemporary, including Napoleon and Beethoven. These add to the powerful atmosphere of the Sculpture Gallery, where the visitor gets a heady sense of the drama of grandiose, monumental works of art evolving from the sculptural body parts displayed around them.

LEFT
Watts at work on the full-scale gesso model of *Tennyson*, c.1899
Adopted by The de Laszlo Foundation

ABOVE
Plaster casts and death masks in the Sculpture Gallery

RIGHT
Detail of *Tennyson*'s hand and hat

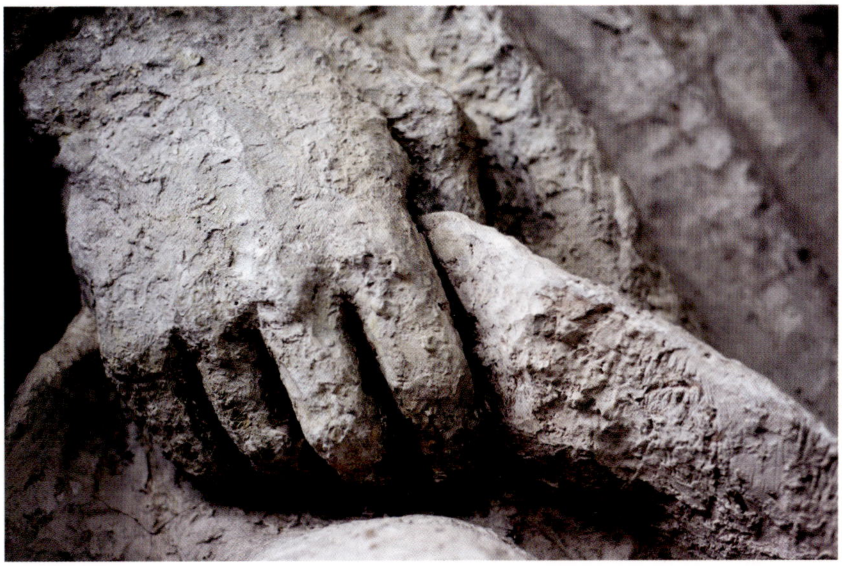

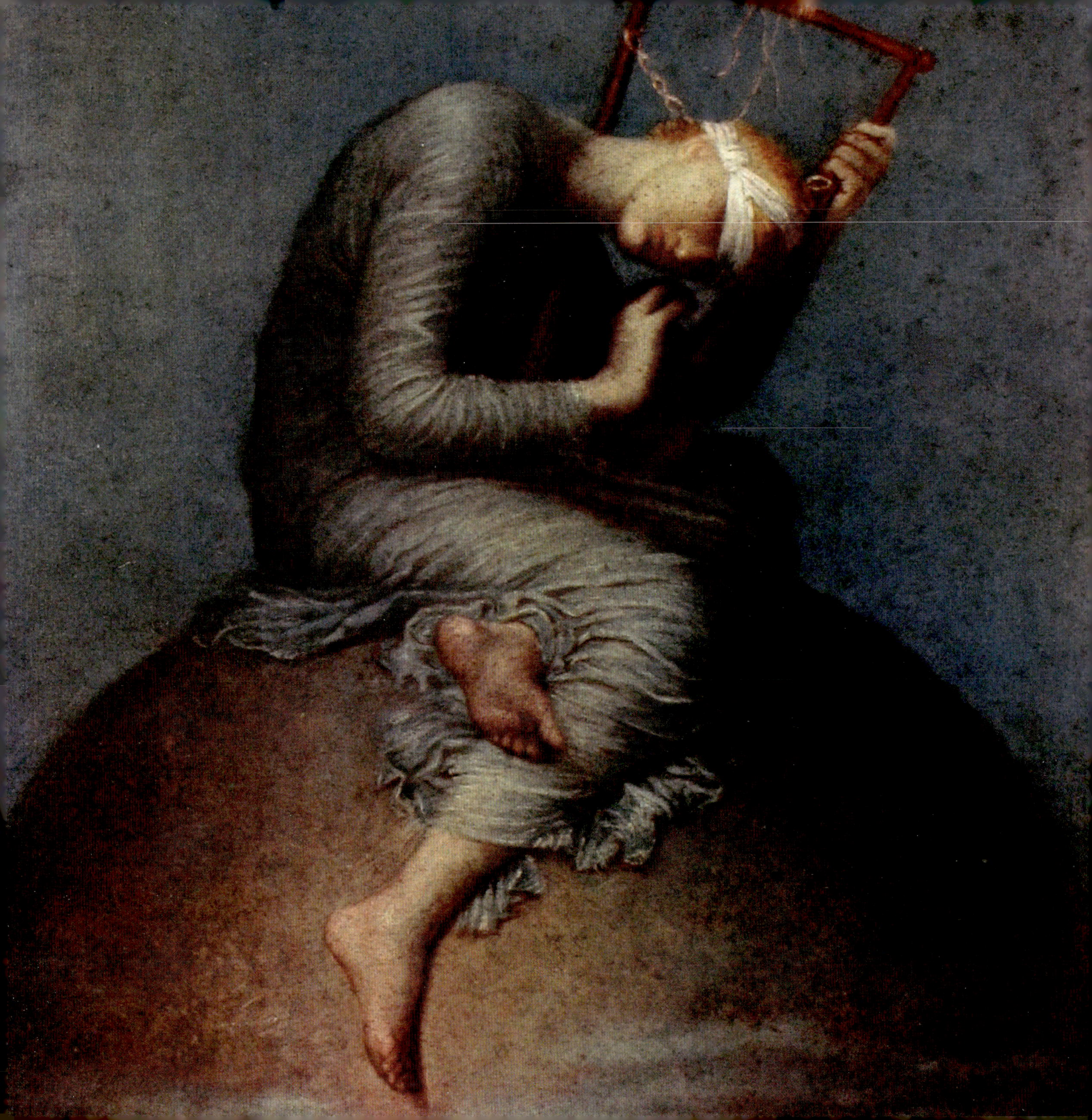

WATTS EXPERIMENTED WITH DRAWING THROUGHOUT HIS VERY LONG CAREER. A KEY PART OF OUR COLLECTION IS MADE UP OF WORKS ON PAPER EXECUTED BY THE ARTIST IN DIFFERENT TECHNIQUES DATING FROM THE 1820s THROUGH TO THE BEGINNING OF THE TWENTIETH CENTURY.

LEFT
Emery Walker, print after G F Watts's painting *Hope* (1885), 1913

PRINTS, DRAWINGS AND PHOTOGRAPHS

Although George Frederic Watts was best known as a painter and sculptor, he was also a prolific and expert draughtsman, producing thousands of studies, sketches and independent drawings throughout his professional career. Watts Gallery's collection of 800 drawings comprises works on paper that span Watts's entire lifetime – from remarkable pencil drawings made when he was only ten years old to sketches produced just weeks before his death at the age of eighty-seven.

Watts first began to draw when he was just a boy, and, as he later wrote to his patron Charles Rickards, "all the early years of my life were given to the study of drawing". From the time he was seven years old, Watts was rarely without a pencil in his hand, and he devoted himself to his drawing exercises and to creating imaginative sketches based on the stories of Sir Walter Scott and other favourite authors.

Watts Gallery holds a number of drawings from this early stage in Watts's artistic training. One particularly impressive example, made when Watts was only eleven years old, is based on a head in Raphael's *Transfiguration*, the Renaissance masterpiece now in the Vatican. Watts's youthful drawing was not copied from the original work but rather from a popular engraving of the painting. Watts faithfully reproduced every line in an effort to train his eye and his hand.

The Gallery's collection also includes numerous figure studies Watts drew of his favourite model, Mary Bartley, a housemaid at Little Holland House where Watts lived as artist-in-residence between 1851 and 1875. According to his biographer and friend Emilie Barrington, Watts said the model had even "more length of limb" than the ancient Greek sculptures he so admired, and he called her Long Mary on account of her beautiful proportions. Watts's drawings of Bartley were not used as direct studies for particular paintings. Instead, the artist created the drawings as reference material that he could consult repeatedly. As Mary Watts recalled: "when painting, Signor referred to the studies made in charcoal on brown paper from this most splendid model … They inspired his work from the first half of the 'sixties to the end of his life".

Some of the most beautiful drawings in the collection were intended as independent artworks in their own right rather than preparatory studies. Watts's large-scale red chalk drawing of *Hope* was produced as his final thought on the theme, after his painted versions of the famous composition were completed. Similarly, Watts's drawing of *Clytie*, made in three different colours of chalk, was probably made as a complement to, rather than as a study for, the more well-known painting and bronze bust of the same subject.

In addition to original drawings by Watts, the Gallery also holds important collections of prints and photographs. One of the ways in which Mary Watts commemorated her husband after his death was to

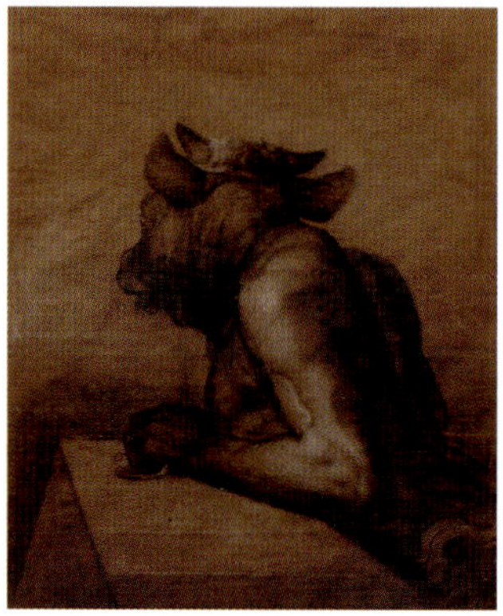

ABOVE
GF Watts, black chalk study for *The Minotaur*, 1885
Adopted by Sir Mark Jones

BELOW
GF Watts, bust-length study of a youth for *Earth*, 1850s
Adopted by the Billmeir Charitable Trust

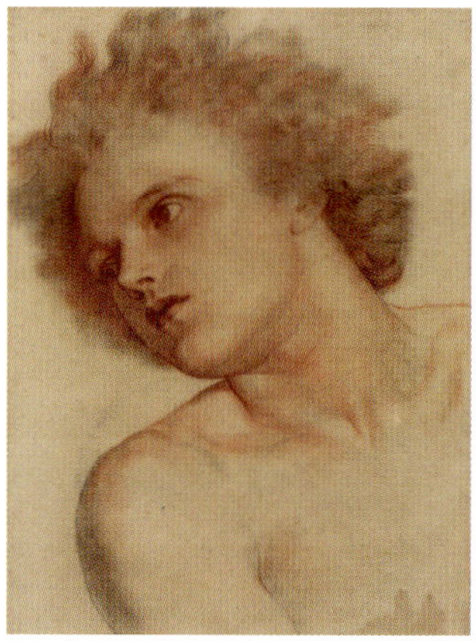

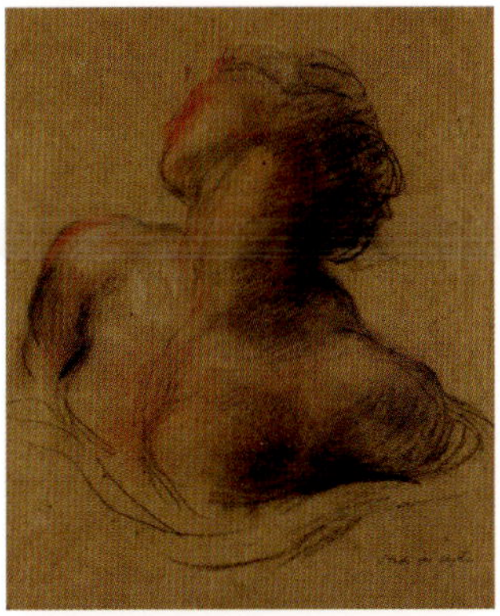

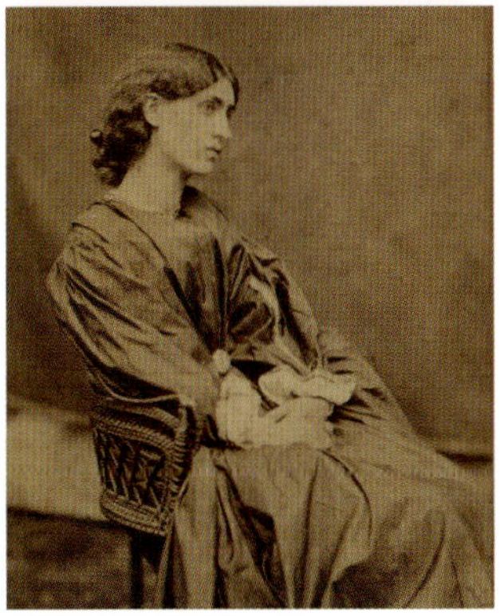

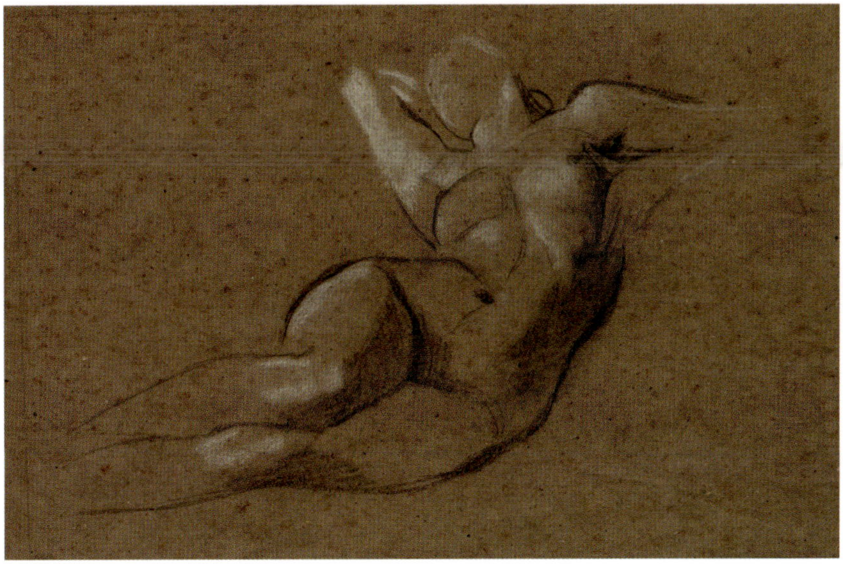

ABOVE (TOP)
GF Watts, chalk study for *Clytie*, 1860s
Adopted by Colin Ford CBE & Sue Grayson Ford MBE

ABOVE (BOTTOM)
Maull & Polyblank, photograph of Jane Morris, 1865

ABOVE (RIGHT)
GF Watts, chalk study of a *Reclining Female Nude*, 1860s

collaborate with the leading printer Emery Walker to produce colour reproductions of his paintings using state-of-the-art photomechanical technology. These prints, which carried Watts's imagery around the world, were published by Mary Watts at Compton.

The Watts Gallery photography collection contains three major groups: images of life at Limnerslease taken by George Andrews, the Wattses' estate steward and amateur photographer; records of Watts's paintings made by Frederic Hollyer, a specialist in fine art photography; and an extraordinary archive of thousands of Victorian photographic portraits collected by the pioneering art dealer Jeremy Maas and generously donated to the Gallery in 2007 by trustee Professor Rob Dickins CBE.

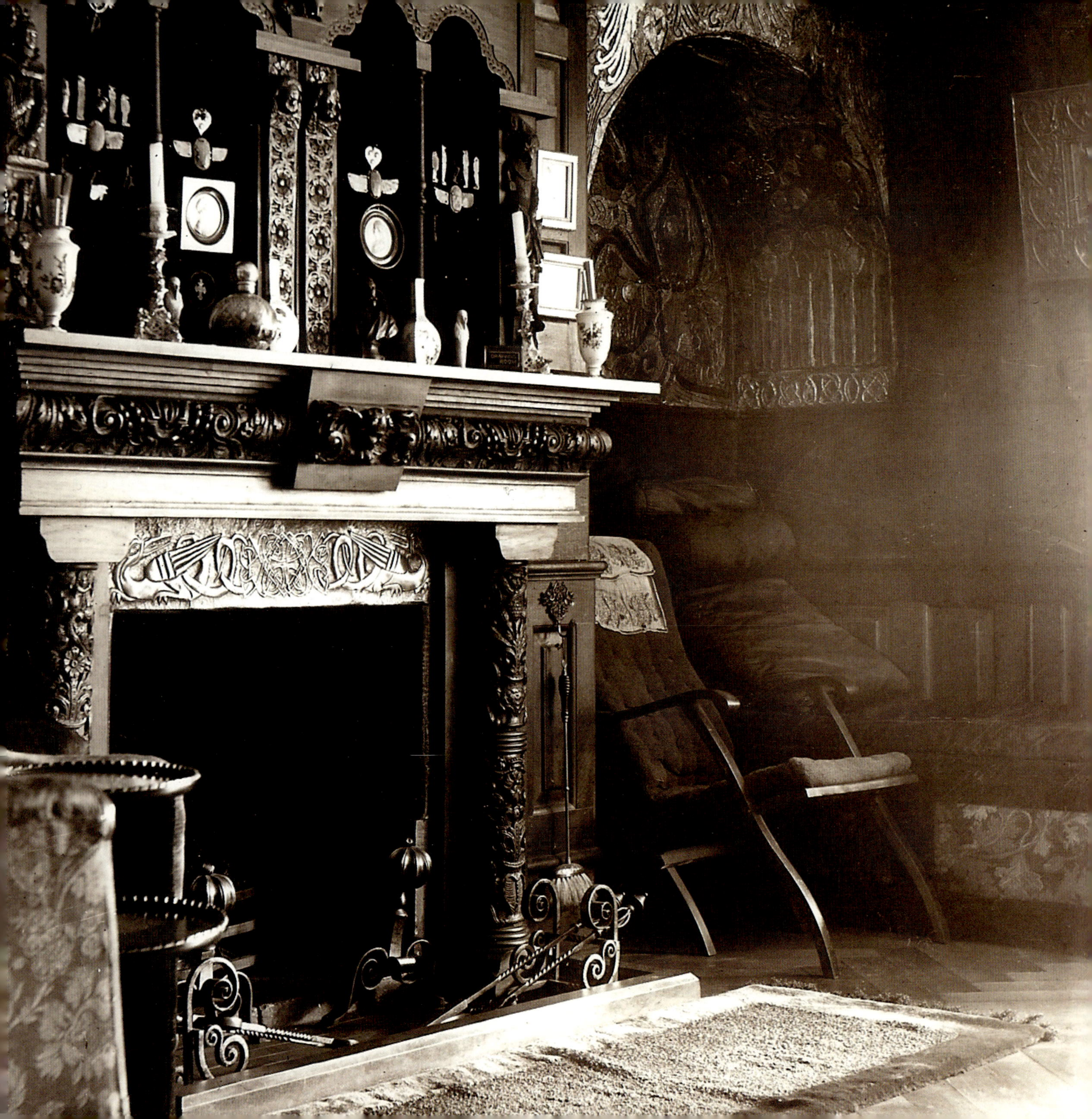

LIMNERSLEASE, AN IMPORTANT ARTS & CRAFTS BUILDING, WAS THE WATTSES' COUNTRY HOME, REFUGE FROM LONDON AND WORKPLACE. THEIR HAPPINESS HERE ENCOURAGED THEM TO GO ON TO CREATE WHAT BECAME AN ARTISTS' VILLAGE. THE WATTS STUDIOS AT LIMNERSLEASE ARE NOW OPEN TO THE PUBLIC.

LEFT
The Niche and fireplace in the Anson Red Room at Limnerslease, 1890s

LIMNERSLEASE AND THE WATTS STUDIOS

George and Mary Watts established a second home at Compton from 1891. The name *Limnerslease* combined the old words *limner* (artist) and *lease* (in the sense of gathering), thus suggesting a late harvest of art for the ageing but still ambitious Watts.

The house stands some three miles south-west of Guildford. Since the 1930s it has found itself next to the A3, but it was originally built on a much older highway – the ancient path between Winchester and Canterbury known as the Pilgrims' Way because of the association of Canterbury with the famous shrine of Thomas Becket.

The Limnerslease estate incorporated, in addition to the main house, a coach-house and a substantial cottage for the gardener. It was also discovered to be home to the remains of an Ancient Roman Villa – further proof that here was a spot planted deep in history.

On Saturday 18 July 1891 George Frederic and Mary Watts entered their new home:

> *We stopped the cabs & walked up ..., Signor stepping in by the drawing room window to take possession, & I following, the blessing hand of the ceiling was over our heads in an instant.*

The ceiling decoration under which they passed, made of low-relief gesso panels, can still be seen in the Hall and Anson Red Room at Limnerslease. The symbols in the Anson Red Room are intended to suggest the joy in work which Mary felt characterised her husband. Mary's imagery here includes the sun, bees, butterflies, birds, wheat and grapes – signifying energy, industry and the fruits of labour.

In the Hall are five even more elaborate large panels representing different spiritual cultures: Buddhism, Hinduism and Judaism from among the living religious traditions; and ancient Assyria and Egypt from antiquity.

I GAVE MY MIND TO THE WHOLE CONCEPTION OF MY CEILING FOR SOME HOURS. IT IS TO BE THE CONCRETE EXPRESSION OF THE SPIRITUAL ATMOSPHERE THAT SIGNOR HAS ROUND HIM – THE AROMA OF HIS THOUGHT PUT INTO THE SILENT LANGUAGE OF SYMBOLS, GRAVEN AS A MEMORIAL OF HIM.

Mary Watts's Diary,
January 1891

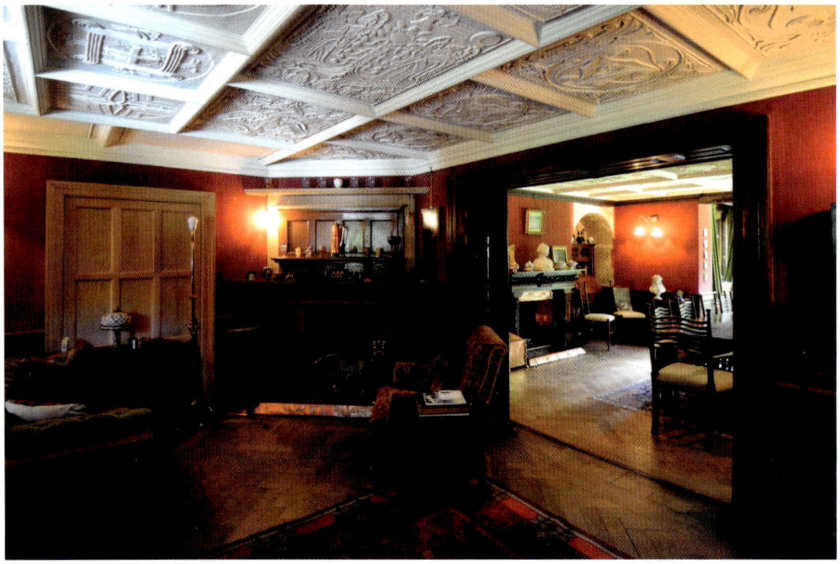

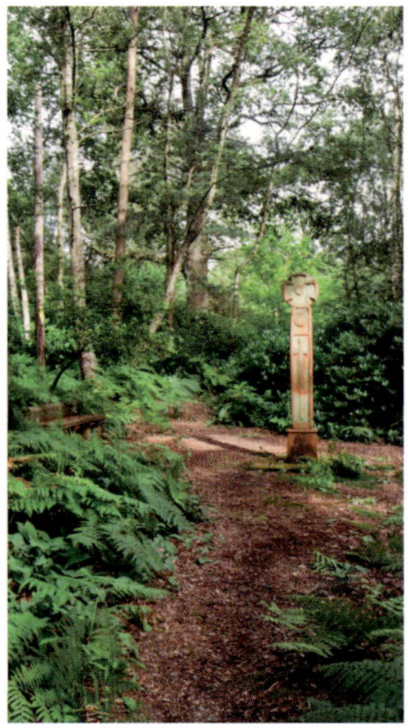

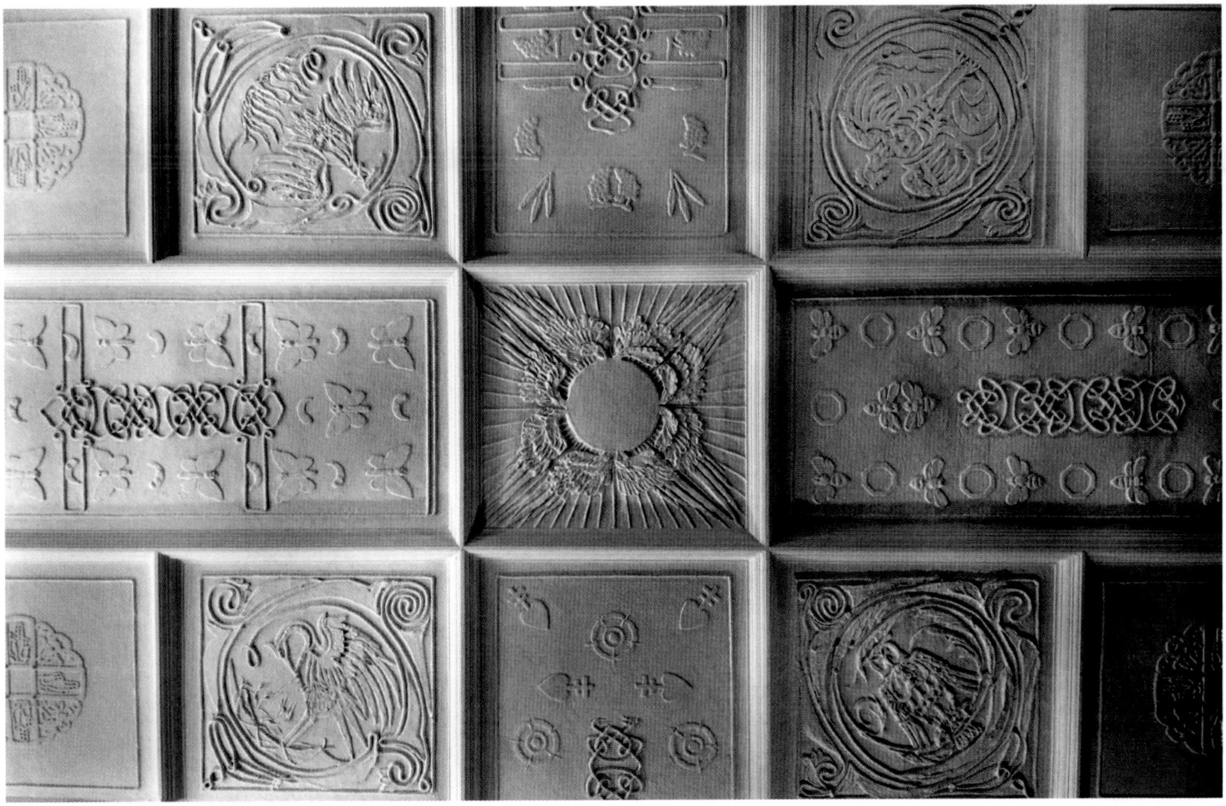

FAR LEFT
The Hall at Limnerslease looking towards the Red Room

LEFT
The Watts Memorial Cross in the Limnerslease woodland

ABOVE
The gesso ceiling in the Red Room of Limnerslease, designed and made by Mary Watts

In 1896 Mary added another series of panels near the windows in the Red Room. Here she used further Celtic patterns and devices along with inscriptions including "The Utmost for the Highest" which Watts had adopted as a personal motto to accompany the design Mary had made for him to use as a seal or bookplate, showing a star reflected in a pool of water. The same words can be seen on one of the lead doors which Mary designed for the Watts Gallery.

The absolute centre of the domestic lives of the Wattses was the arched recess beside the fireplace in the Red Room which they called their 'Niche'. This was their cosy evening corner, where Mary would read to the slightly deaf Watts. Often her diary suggests that

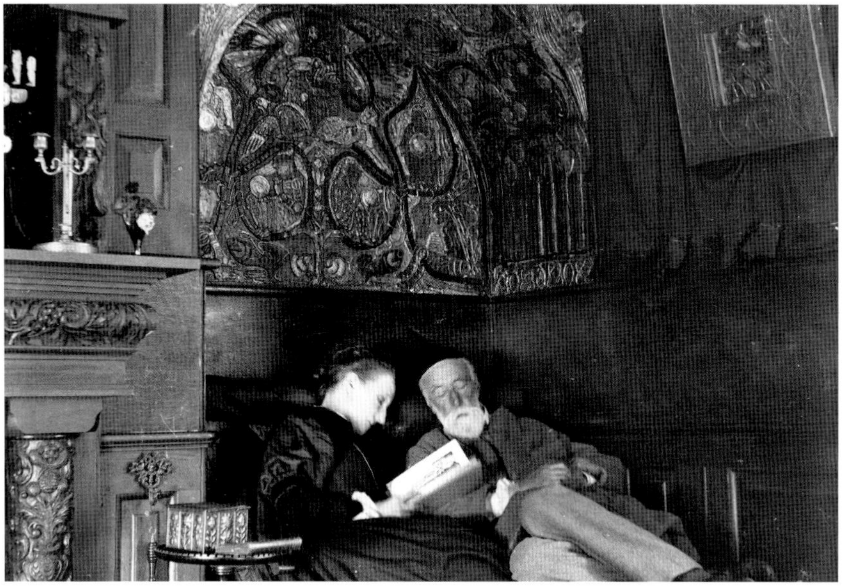

Mary looked forward more than anything to the hours they spent here reading everything from Jane Austen to Tolstoy, from the latest philosophies of religion to new scientific discoveries.

Mary was appropriately very particular about the decoration of the Niche, completed in 1893 but now very sadly lost, using richly painted gesso relief, in styles derived from early medieval manuscript illumination and other Celtic art.

The architect of Limnerslease was Ernest George who ran a large London practice in which many important architects such as Edwin Lutyens trained. The house is in a picturesque Arts & Crafts idiom. It was a place for work and relaxation – not for impressing or throwing parties. Nevertheless, among the many famous visitors were the sisters Virginia Woolf and Vanessa Bell, whose family Watts had known for many years.

The most active part of the house was on the eastern side, where both artists had their studios. G F Watts's studio – now restored and

SIGNOR ASKED ME WHAT I WAS DESIGNING FOR THE NICHE. I SAID I WANT IT TO BE DESCRIPTIVE OF THE TIME WE PASS THERE – THE THINGS WE THINK OF CHIEFLY – THEREFORE I AM TRYING TO MAKE MY PATTERNS EXPRESS THE WHOLE RANGE. FLOWERS, TREES, BIRDS, BEASTS & MAN IN HIS DOUBLE NATURE – SPIRIT & FLESH – SUN, STARS, MOON – ANGELS – & A LIGHT BEYOND FROM WHOM THEY VEIL THEIR FACES! BUT THAT IS NOT ALL: PAPYRUS COMES IN FOR BOOKS, POPPIES FOR REST – & THEN I AM TRYING TO GET IN PAINTING, ART, SCIENCE, RELIGION, HISTORY, FICTION. HE LAUGHED: "OH, YOU ARE GREEDY" HE SAID. MY PRESENT IDEA IS TO MAKE IT A KIND OF ILLUMINATION IF I CAN.

Mary Watts's Diary, February 1893

FAR LEFT
Mary Watts reading to GF Watts in the Niche at Limnerslease

BELOW LEFT
The Studio at Limnerslease

BELOW RIGHT
Watts sitting in front of his painting *The Court of Death*

from 2016 open to the public – is a very striking space, tall in relation to its width, rather like a Renaissance chapel. Fittingly for such an atmosphere, the painting which dominated the studio for the first decade of its existence was Watts's *The Court of Death*, his vast version of a Renaissance altarpiece in which the traditional Madonna is replaced by a beautiful personification of Death. So large is this picture that a special hatch was let into the floor so that it could be raised and lowered to allow Watts to reach all of its surface.

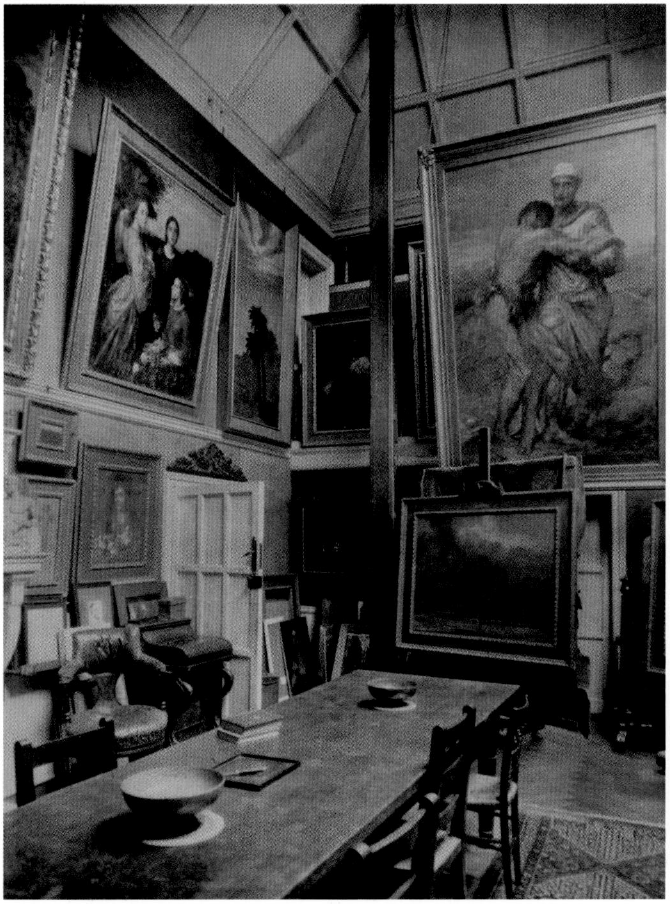

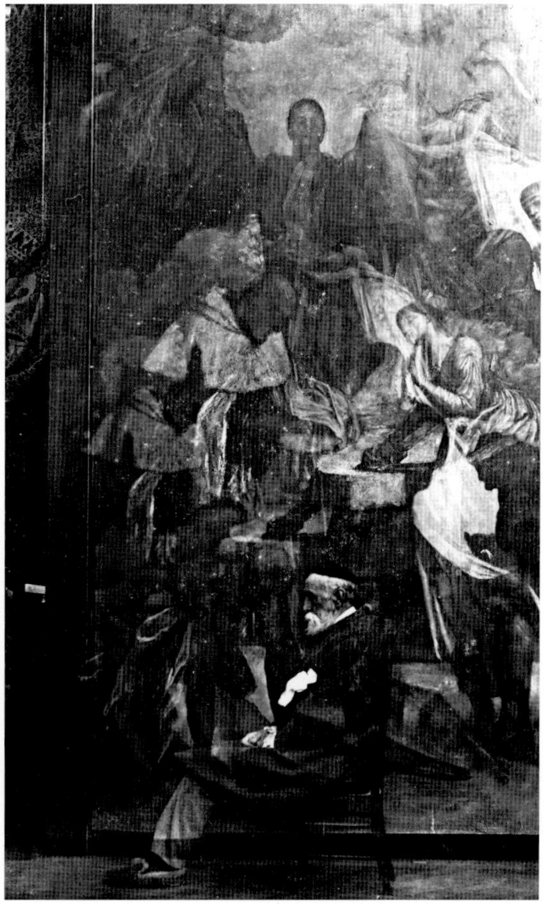

Mary Watts used the next-door room as her studio. Now the Mary Watts Gallery, this was where much of the communal creativity of Limnerslease took place – where notable visiting musicians such as the great Hungarian violinist Joseph Joachim would play; where Mary taught her Thursday evening terracotta classes for local villagers; and where, from 1898, she would create much of the interior decoration of the Watts Chapel.

The Wattses' domestic contentment (supported by a staff of five female servants) depended primarily on one another, but also on a large extended family of relations, including Mary's sisters and their children, and on their Compton neighbours, whose children were invited for regular parties. Mary's diary records a party in May 1898 which involved the young people playing at the newly marketed game of Piladex, which involved batting a kind of balloon back and forth along a string. Watching the fun was "Signor, sitting beside us & laughing at the shouts & screams & stamps. Afterwards a game of Old Maid & he played too, to the children's great delight".

MY CLASS! WE WERE PREPARED FOR 40, BUT 48 SWARMED IN, & NEARLY OVERWHELMED US, ALL GOOD & WELL MANNERED – SO HAPPY TO BE AT WORK AGAIN – I GOT THROUGH IT WELL.

Mary Watts's Diary, February 1898

BELOW LEFT
View of Limnerslease

BELOW RIGHT
G F Watts reclining on a daybed

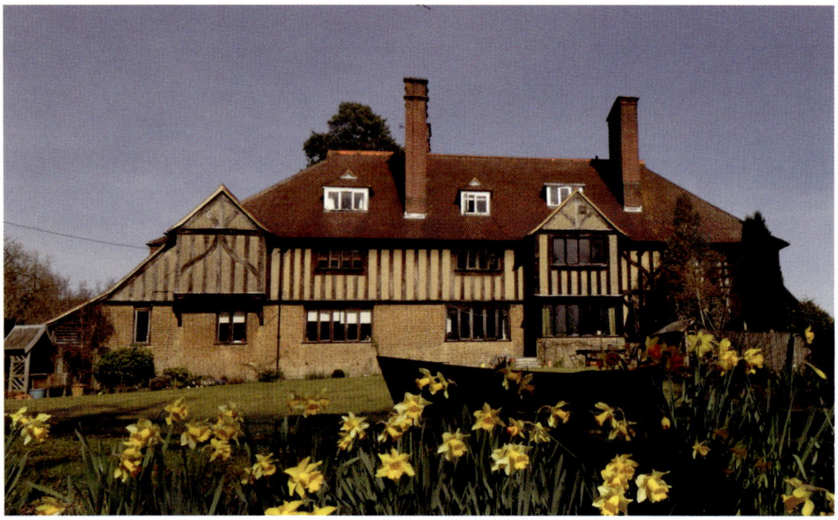

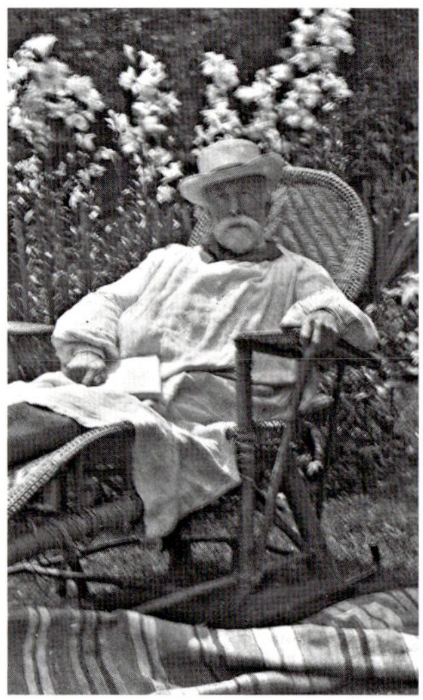

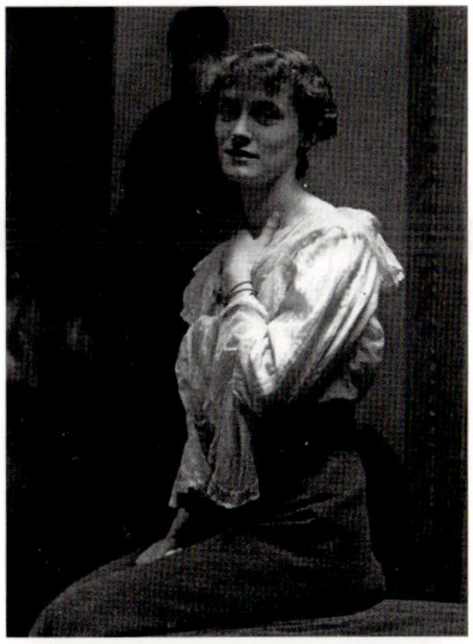

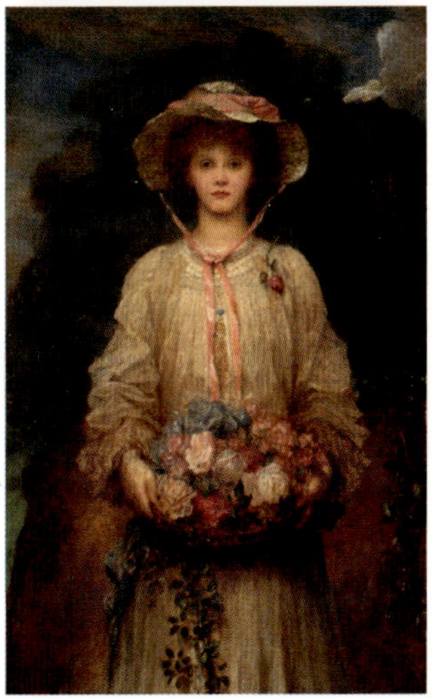

From 1898 the Wattses were joined by Lilian Macintosh, their ward, and eventually heir. Lily had long been known to Mary: as an orphan she had gone to live with Mary's sister and her husband. But with her elfin good looks and tender nature, she seemed to suit the artistic culture of the Wattses' world, and gradually she came to form the third member of their family.

Following Mary's death in 1938 much of the contents of Limnerslease was sold and the estate divided into different properties. During the Second World War the house was taken over by Ardente, a company producing radar and sonar equipment for the Navy. The Compton Pottery finally closed in 1956.

In 2011 a remarkable opportunity arose when all parts of the house came onto the market at the same time, affording Watts Gallery Trust a unique chance to acquire Limnerslease, to save it for the nation and reunite it with the Watts Gallery and Watts Chapel and Cemetery. In 2016 the Watts Studios at Limnerslease opened to the public, allowing everyone the chance to visit the studios of GF and Mary Watts, as well as the Compton Gallery, which tells the story of the Wattses' lives at Compton, and a Conservation Studio and a space for learning activities of all levels. Our long-term campaign to be able to open all of Limnerslease to the public continues.

TOP
Lilian Macintosh, ward of George and Mary Watts

BOTTOM
GF Watts, *Lilian*, 1904
Adopted by David Davis, Chairman, Surrey County Council

THE SURREY HOME WAS AN UNQUALIFIED SUCCESS. SUCH A HOME, HE SAID, WAS WHAT HE NEVER THOUGHT TO POSSESS, AND HIS ENJOYMENT OF IT WAS LIKE THE ENJOYMENT OF A CHILD, AS MY SISTER SAID WHEN HE CALLED TO US TO COME AND HEAR HOW DELIGHTFUL THE SOUND OF THE WIND WAS AMONG THE TREES.

Mary Watts, *Annals of an Artist's Life*, 1912

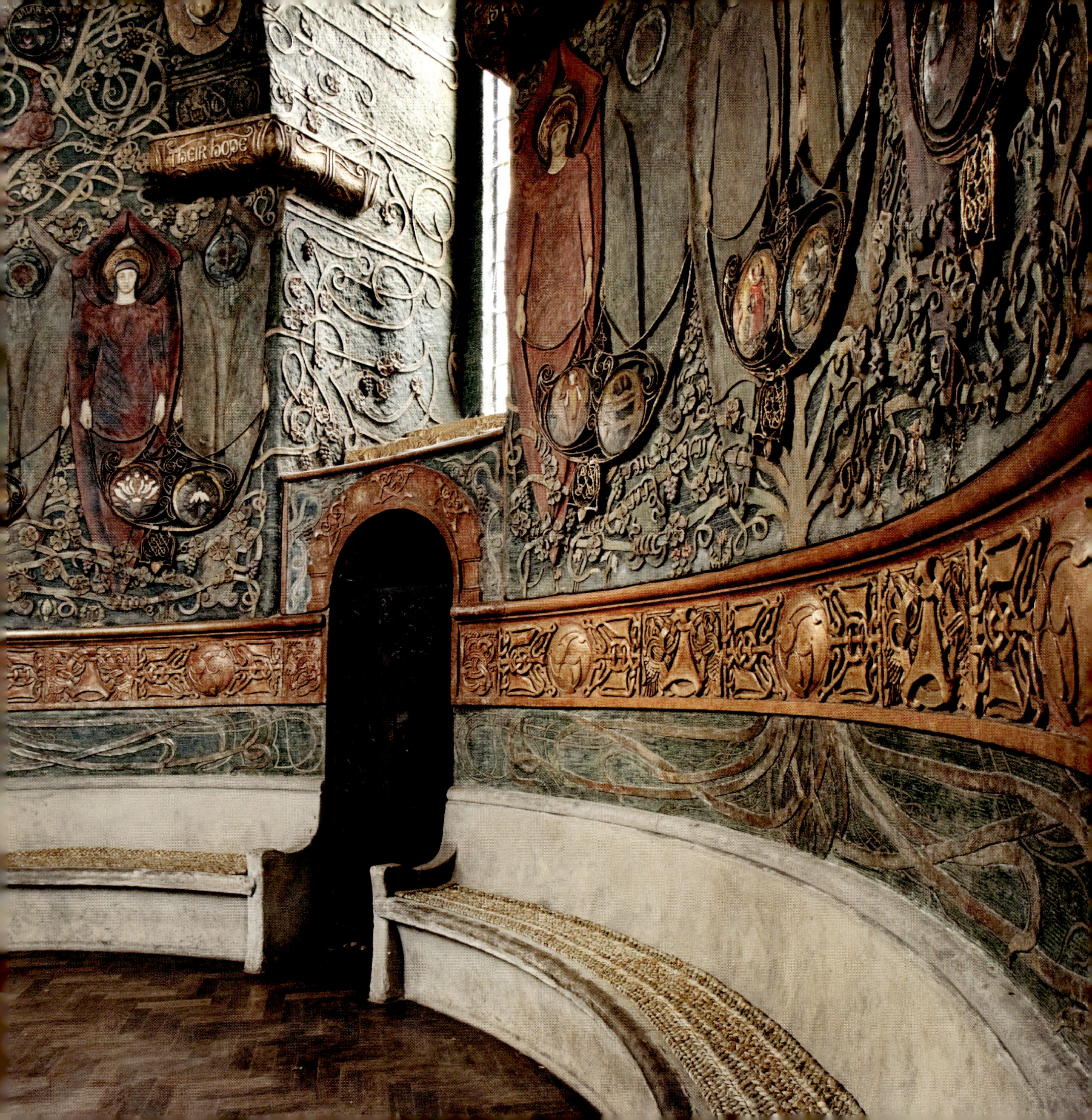
THEIR HOPE

THE WATTS CHAPEL IS THE MASTERPIECE OF MARY WATTS. BUILT AS THE CENTREPIECE OF A NEW VILLAGE CEMETERY, IT WAS CREATED AND DECORATED ENTIRELY BY LOCAL PEOPLE UNDER MARY'S GUIDANCE. THE CHAPEL IS RECOGNISED AS ONE OF THE MOST IMPORTANT ART NOUVEAU BUILDINGS IN BRITAIN.

LEFT
Interior of the Watts Chapel

WATTS CHAPEL AND CEMETERY

The Watts Chapel, built on Budborough Hill by Mary Watts and the villagers of Compton between 1895 and 1904, is one of the most extraordinary small buildings in England. From the outside it looks like a Byzantine or Orthodox church bizarrely transplanted from Eastern Europe to a Surrey hillside. Inside, the visitor feels as if they have been dropped into a lusciously decorated capsule. The Chapel was constructed for use in the funerals of Compton villagers, and although today managed by Watts Gallery Trust, remains the property of the Compton Parish Council and is very much still in use, as is the Watts Cemetery in which it stands.

Not long after the Wattses moved to Compton, the village bought land near to Limnerslease to create a cemetery to supplement the graveyard of the exquisite medieval village church, St Nicholas. Mary Watts saw her chance to take her ambitions as a designer to an entirely new level, and offered, along with her husband as financial backer, to build for the village a mortuary chapel (a consecrated space where the bodies of the dead lie briefly before burial or cremation).

In 1895 Mary began a weekly class at Limnerslease, training local people in the making of terracotta panels to decorate the exterior of the chapel with a complex scheme of symbols deriving from Celtic, Romanesque, Jewish and Egyptian traditions. She also recruited a small number of trained craftsmen to oversee the decorative work.

The Chapel was built using small bricks from a brickworks in nearby Guildford. The area had many of these in the nineteenth century, due to a local seam of red clay. It is the dimensions of the bricks that gives the tall, narrow Chapel its Byzantine look, along with its basic plan – a circle intersected by a cross. Mary discovered a seam of the red clay in the grounds of Limnerslease itself, and was able to put this to use for the terracotta decorations of the Chapel walls.

So elaborate and multi-layered is the decoration that it is impossible to describe it succinctly. Clearly, however, while certainly still Christian, the patterning expresses Mary's belief that the symbolic systems of different historical civilisations could be synthesised into a universal language of fundamental human concerns.

"The Path of the Just" is how Mary described the walk around the circular exterior of the Chapel, taking this image from the Book of Proverbs. Four friezes show positive human characteristics, each illustrated by a variety of scrolling patterns, angels and birds. The Path of Truth shows the owl, symbolic of wisdom, while the Path of Hope has the peacock, which loses its wonderful tail feathers in autumn and grows them again the following spring. The bird on the Path of Light is the eagle, that sees further than any other bird; and, finally, the Path of Love shows the pelican, traditionally a symbol of selfless devotion.

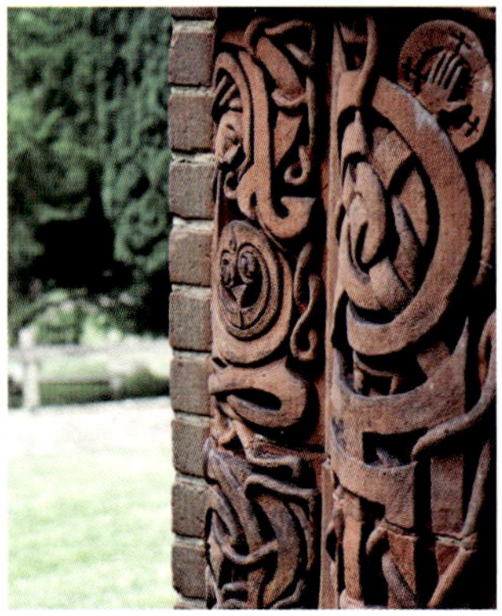

ABOVE
Decoration next to the Chapel doorway

RIGHT
The Watts Chapel exterior

AS FAR AS IS POSSIBLE THEREFORE EVERY BIT OF THE DECORATION OF THIS CHAPEL, MODELLED IN CLAY OF SURREY, BY COMPTON HANDS, UNDER UNUSUAL CONDITIONS – MUCH OF THE WORK HAVING BEEN DONE GRATUITOUSLY, AND ALL OF IT WITH THE LOVE THAT MADE THE WORK DELIGHTFUL – HAS SOMETHING TO SAY, THOUGH THE PATTERNS CAN CLAIM TO BE NO MORE THAN THE LETTERS OF A GREAT WORD.

Mary Watts, *The Word in the Pattern*, 1905

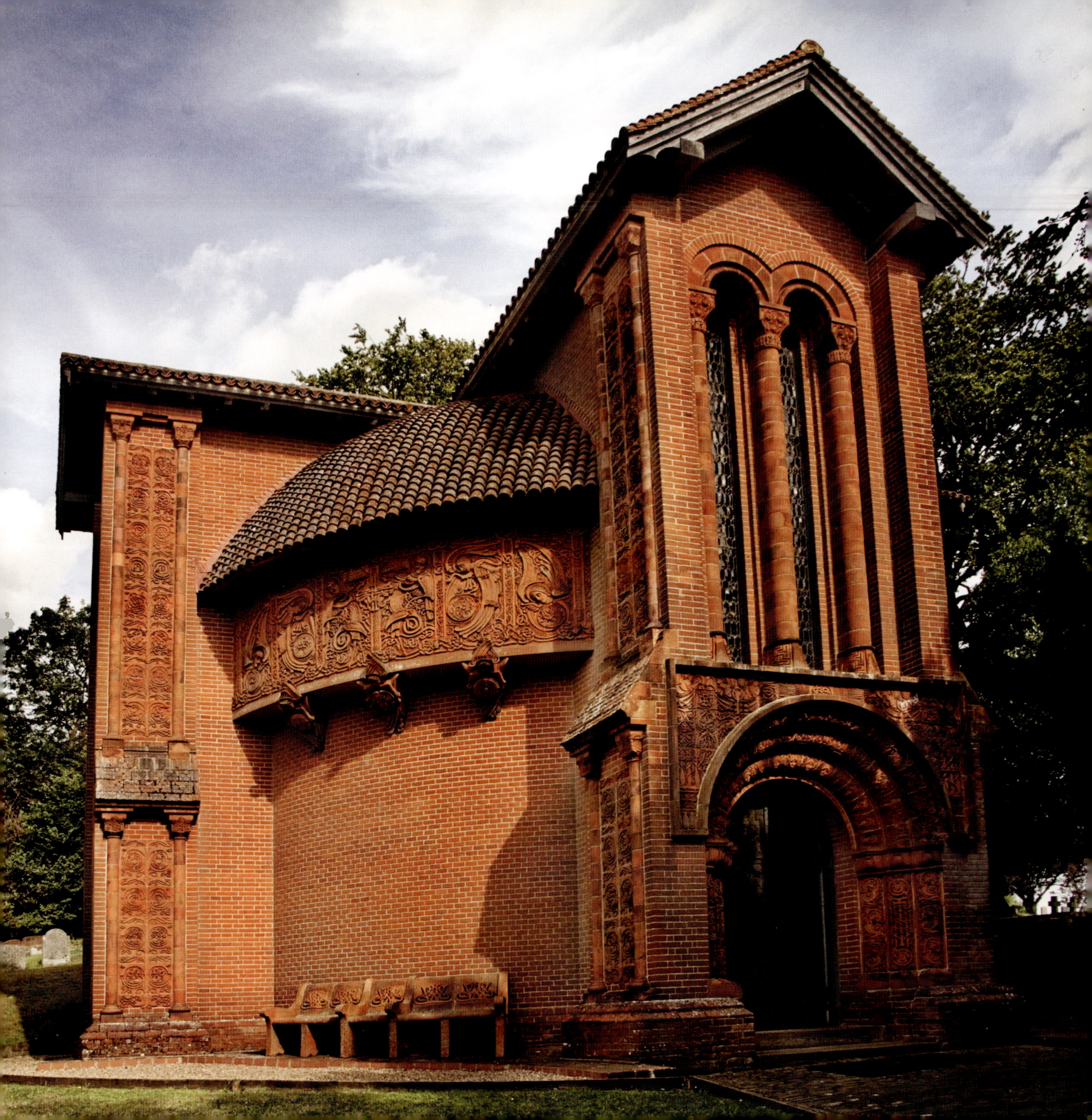

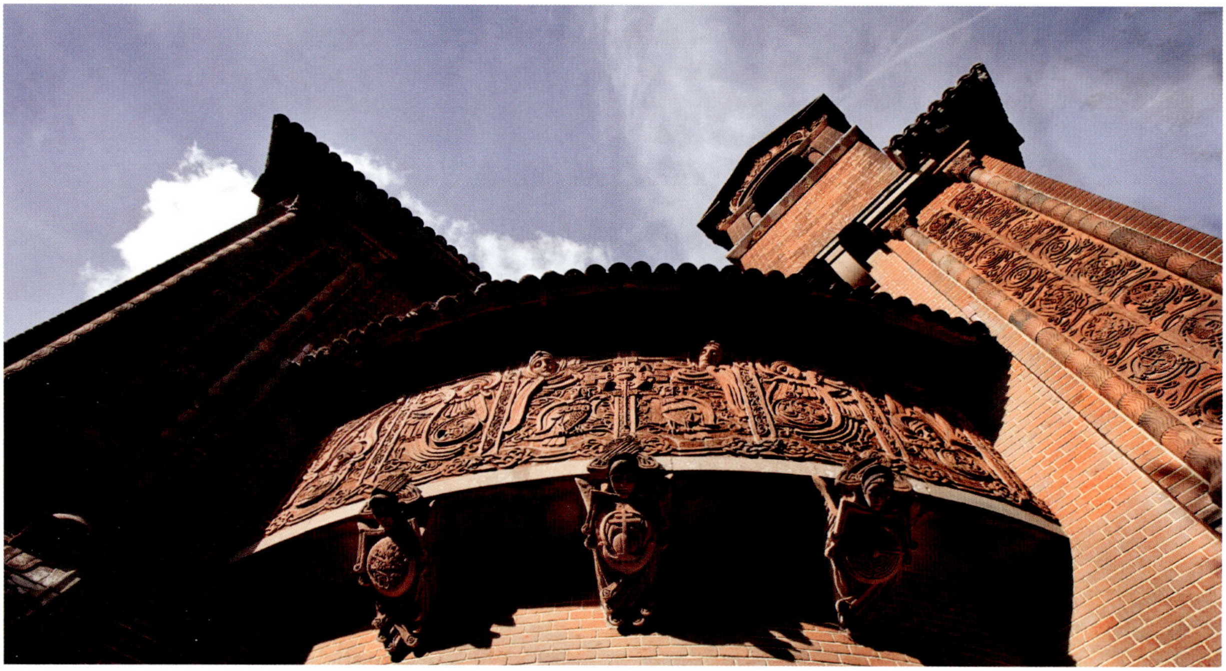

On the buttresses quartering the Chapel are ascending sequences of organic forms describing the Tree of Life, "a climbing creation" in Mary's words, "rising from flower to fruit, from shell to fish, serpent, beast, bird."

The beautiful doors were carved by the Compton carpenter, Thomas Steadman, and its hinges made by the local blacksmith Clarence Sex. Surrounding the entrance are an arch and pillars decorated with clay tiles, illustrating the sadness inevitable in a cemetery combined with hope of renewal. Angels alternately look down in sorrow and up in hope, while faces on the pillars "learn truths from nature", admiring little miracles such as a butterfly emerging from a chrysalis, and flowers appearing from scattered seeds.

The Watts Chapel was consecrated in July 1898 by the Bishop of Winchester: a contemporary photograph shows G F Watts, among others, greeting him at the cemetery's lychgate. No sooner was this

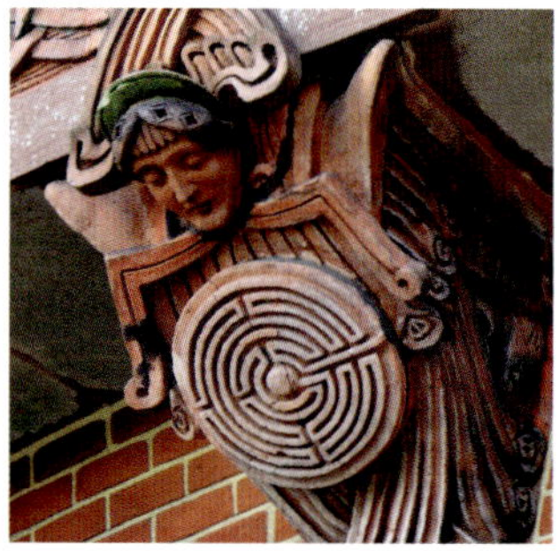

TOP
Decoration on the exterior of the Watts Chapel showing one of the friezes with the Tree of Life motif on the buttresses

ABOVE
Corbel figure with maze, symbolising the difficult path through life

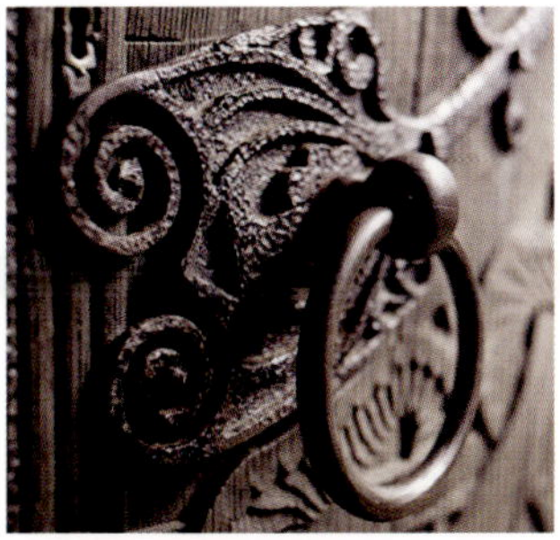

ceremony complete than Mary resumed her classes at Limnerslease to begin the decoration of the interior of the Chapel. Much of this was made up of large panels carrying plaster designs in low relief. Further detailing was picked out in felt, rope and other materials – with the whole scheme painted in the richest colours.

Throughout the interior scheme, the tendrils of another Tree of Life bring organic unity to a potentially overwhelming experience. Dominating the lower part of the inside of the Chapel are pairs of angels, or divine messengers, who alternately face or turn away from the visitor, "presenting the light or the dark side of all things" so as to "suggest the earthly conditions in which the soul of man finds itself". Each pair of angels has at their base two discs containing illustrations of contrasting principles such as Growth and Decay, Labour and Rest or the Real and the Ideal.

Over the messengers are four magnificent Seraphs, the noblest of the angels. The winged children's heads are described by Mary as representing human souls, while at the centre of the roof is "the circle of the Eternal – without beginning, without end".

ABOVE
Chapel door detail

BELOW LEFT
Doorway of the Chapel

BELOW RIGHT
GF and Mary Watts with the Bishop of Winchester at the lychgate before the procession to the Chapel for its consecration on 1 July 1898

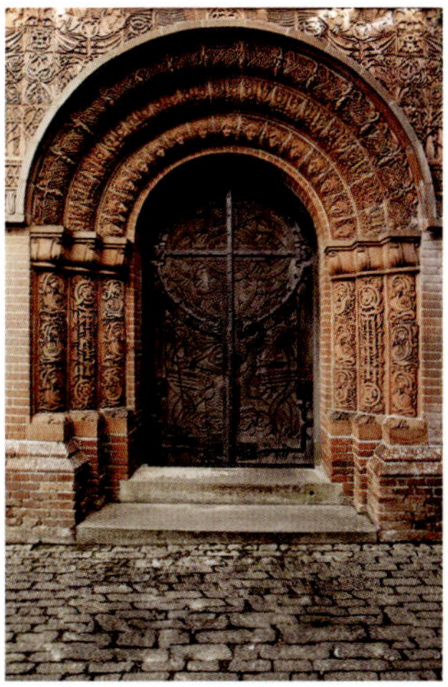

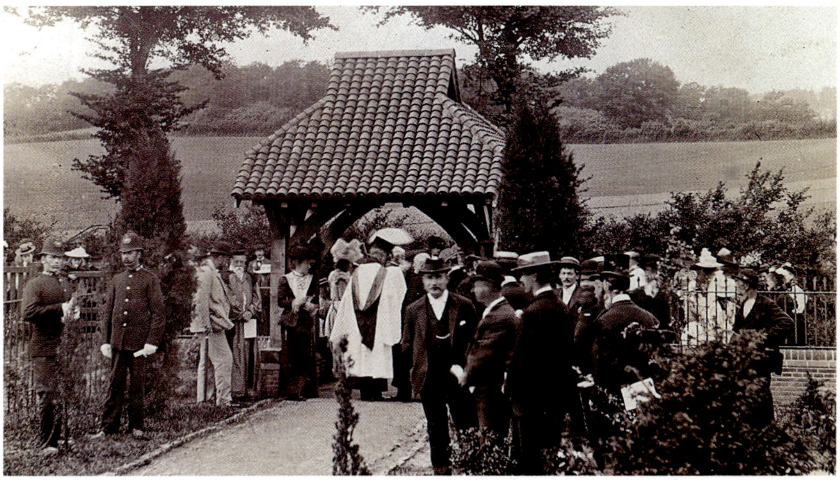

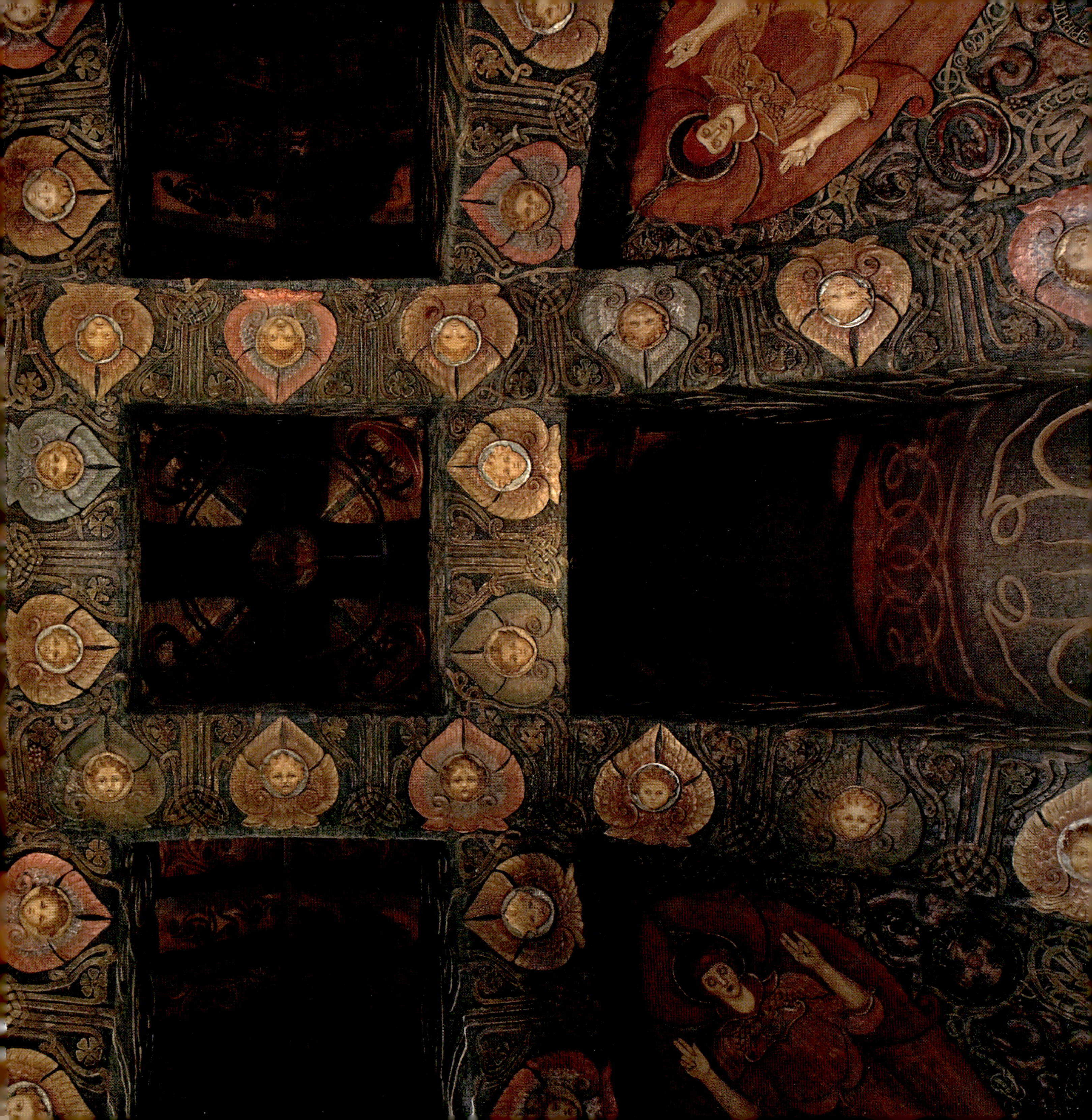

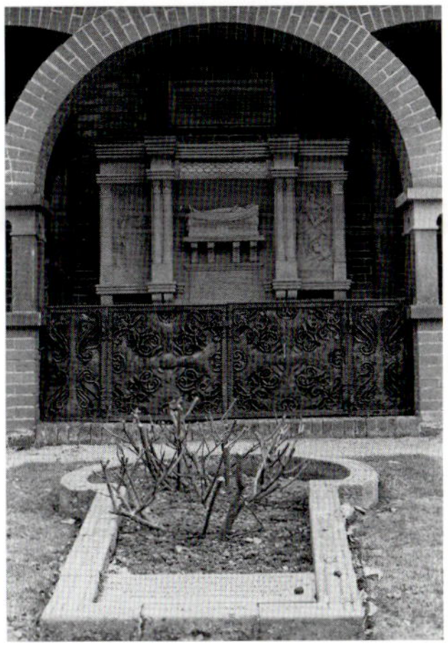

ABOVE
Memorial to GF Watts in the Cemetery Cloister with the grave of GF and Mary Watts in the foreground

LEFT
The Watts Chapel ceiling

RIGHT
View of the Chapel from the Cloister

The Watts Chapel was fully completed in 1904. The finishing touch was the installation of the painting over the altar – *The All-Pervading* by GF Watts.

Watts died in London on 1 July 1904. The casket containing his ashes was displayed in the Chapel and then interred in the cemetery. His grave is strikingly modest – a simple keyhole-shaped kerb with a birdbath (well suited given his passion for bird-life) in Celtic style. Apart from the writer Aldous Huxley (whose ashes joined those of other members of his family in the 1960s) there are no other historical celebrities in the Watts Cemetery. It has always fulfilled the role intended for it, as a final resting place for local people. As Mary, whose own ashes joined those of her husband in 1938, put it, the Chapel was "Built to the loving memory of all who find rest near its walls, and for the comfort and help of those to whom the sorrow of separation yet remains."

THE WATTS CEMETERY IS HOME TO A RICH ARRAY OF RARE WILD FLOWERS, INCLUDING SMOOTH HAWK'S-BEARD, IVY-LEAVED SPEEDWELL AND CREEPING CINQUEFOIL.

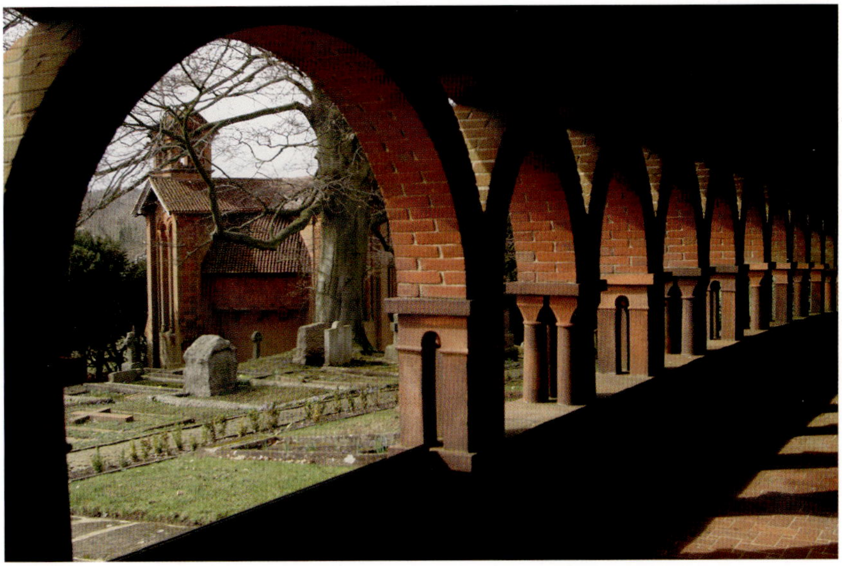

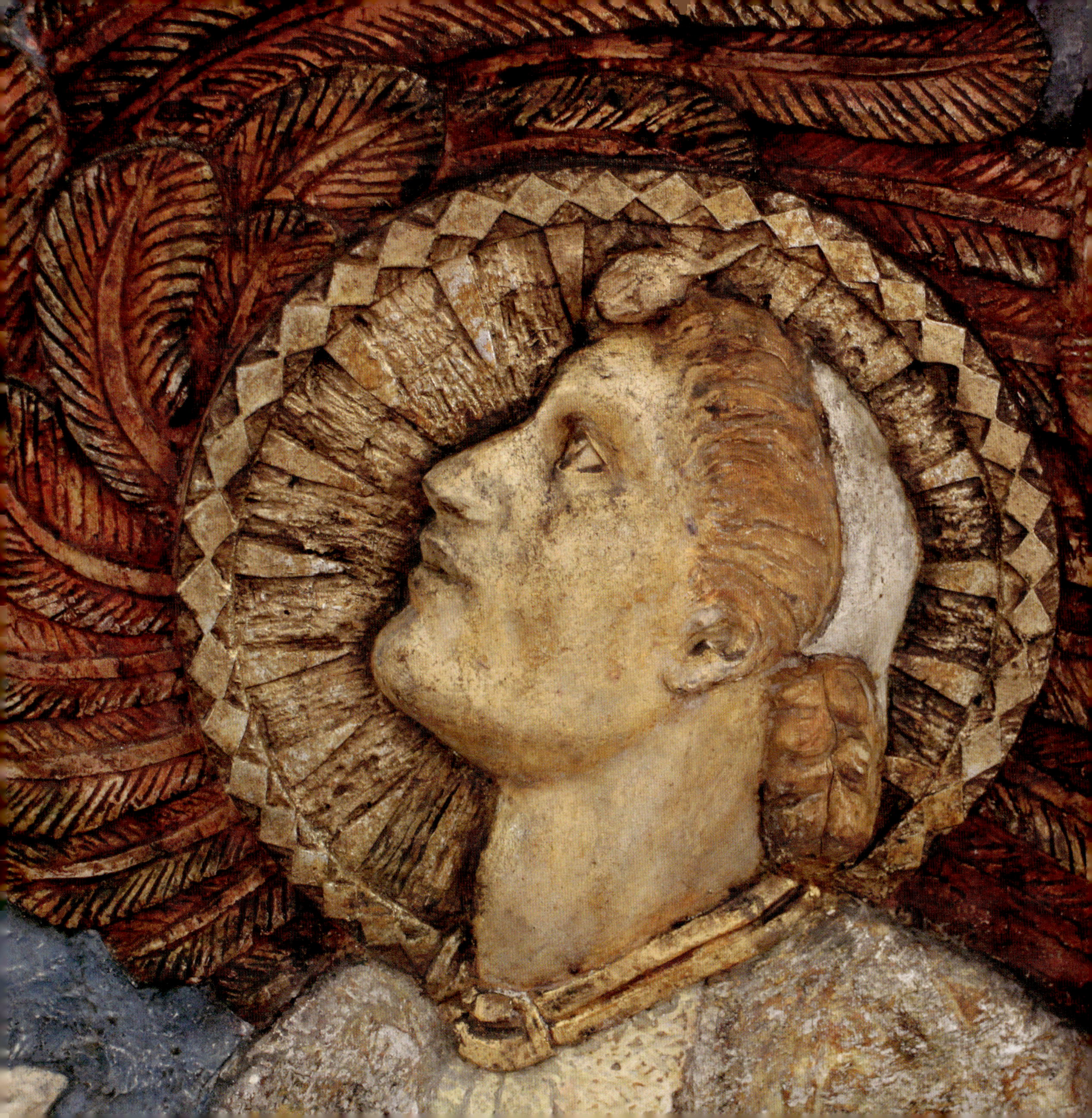

FOLLOWING THE LEAD OF VICTORIAN SOCIAL REFORMERS SUCH AS WILLIAM MORRIS AND JOHN RUSKIN, MARY WATTS ESTABLISHED THE COMPTON POTTERS' ARTS GUILD IN 1898 TO PROMOTE TRADITIONAL HANDICRAFTS AMONG THE LOCAL COMMUNITY. THEIR PRODUCTS WERE SOLD THROUGH FASHIONABLE RETAILERS SUCH AS LIBERTY AND ARE STILL FAMILIAR AND POPULAR TODAY.

LEFT
Mary Watts and the Compton Potters' Arts Guild, detail from the decoration for the Cambridge Military Hospital, Aldershot c.1916–21

MARY WATTS AND THE COMPTON POTTERY

Once the Watts Chapel had been consecrated in 1898, Mary Watts began a new regular evening class at Limnerslease with the intention of executing the interior decoration of the Chapel. But her local collaborators had become so enthusiastic about their work in terracotta that Mary felt ready to develop, in addition, a fully-fledged pottery business on the back of the Chapel project. The plan soon adopted was to emphasise decorative, artistic pieces, subsidised by more lucrative commissions for gravestones and sundials.

The bottle-shaped wood-fired kiln, designed by William De Morgan, that had been constructed in the grounds of Limnerslease was set working again. Memorials for the Watts Cemetery – and further afield – were soon in production, as were the sundials set on pedestals still to be found in gardens across southern England. By 1901 Mary had recruited a full-time pottery manager, James Nicol, who was to remain her lieutenant until 1930,

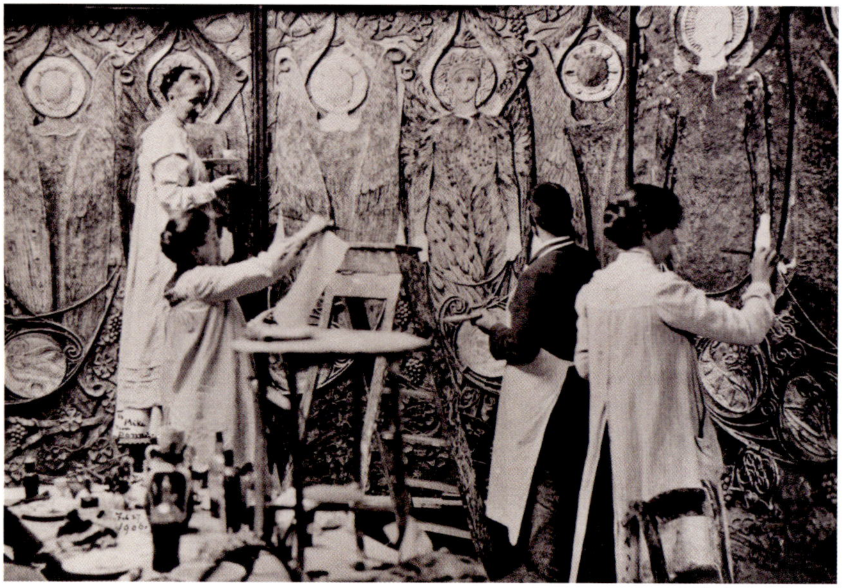

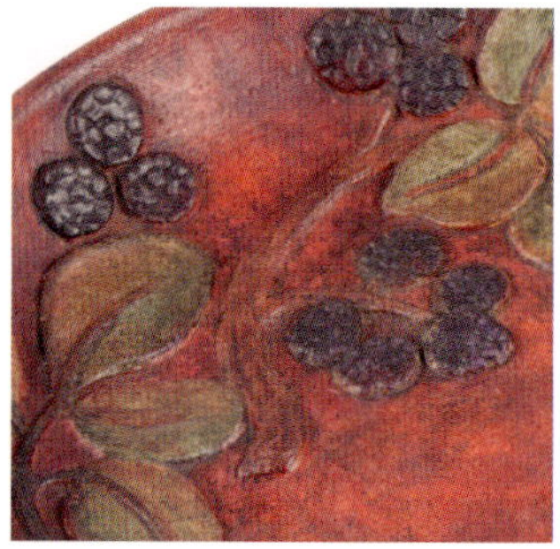

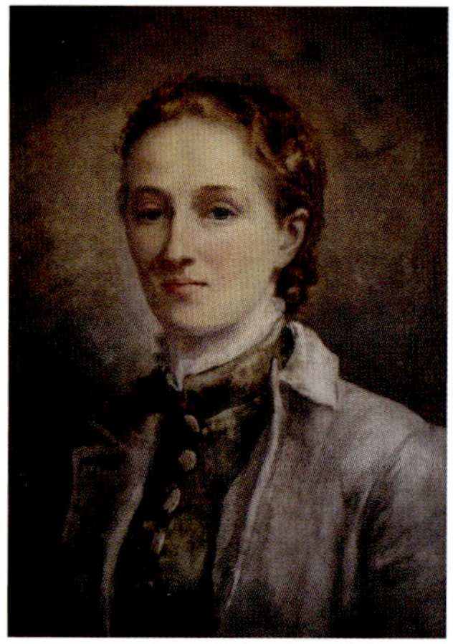

living in a cottage near the premises. A site across Down Lane from Limnerslease was acquired for the Pottery Building where in due course a larger kiln was constructed.

By 1904, when the Watts Picture Gallery opened with accommodation for the pottery apprentices, the establishment became the Compton Potters' Arts Guild. The name reflects the ideals of William Morris and John Ruskin who advocated a return to the pride in communal workmanship of pre-industrial times.

Compton Pottery is still associated especially with its locally-sourced terracotta, although later it produced more dainty objects in lighter commercial clay. Most distinctive of all are the chunky garden pots which are now so highly valued once more. These were typically press-moulded (the red clay was shaped by being pressed into plaster moulds), but some were thrown on the potter's wheel with the decoration then added separately. The fondly remembered *Potter's Wheel* BBC interlude film of the early 1950s shows the hands

ABOVE LEFT
Mary Watts and her collaborators decorating interior panels for the Chapel, c.1902

ABOVE (TOP)
Compton Pottery Blackberry Bowl, 1920s/30s

ABOVE (BOTTOM)
Mary Watts, *Self-Portrait*, 1882

of Compton potter George Aubertin.

Finished pots were laid out for sale outside the pottery, next to the horse-turned pug-mill used to prepare the raw clay for working. The pots were also sold through other outlets, most notably Liberty of London, where Mary was named as their designer – against the famous store's regular policy of marketing only under their own brandname. Liberty also sold an elegant brooch based on one of Mary's key Chapel motifs, and exhibited the Celtic-patterned Pelican rug which she designed to be manufactured by Alexander Morton & Co. at Killibegs, County Donegal in Ireland.

Watts Gallery – Artists' Village offers various opportunities to see the work of Mary Watts and the Compton Pottery. At the Watts Studios at Limnerslease there is a dedicated Mary Watts Gallery which explores the creation of the Watts Chapel and which also gives visitors the chance to appreciate Mary's many other achievements.

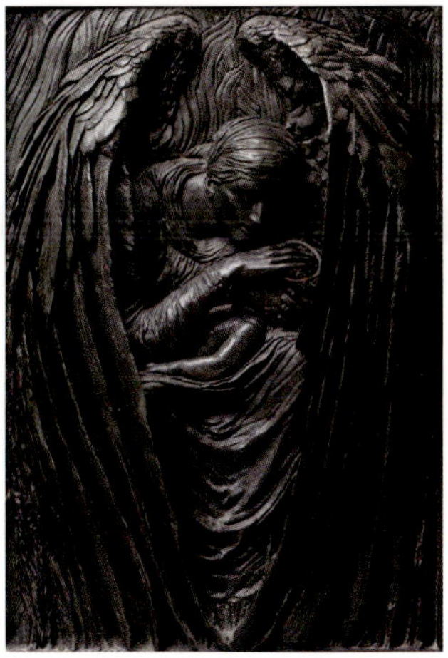

ABOVE
Central Panel of the Commemorative Bronze Relief Triptych designed by Mary Watts after GF Watts's paintings

Photograph by John Hammond

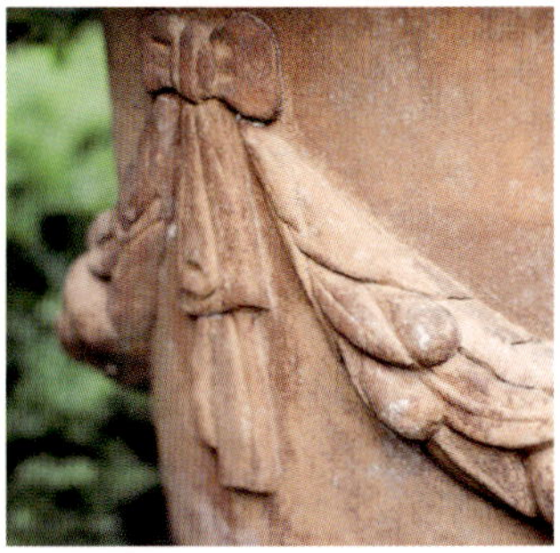

ABOVE
Detail of a Compton Pottery garden pot

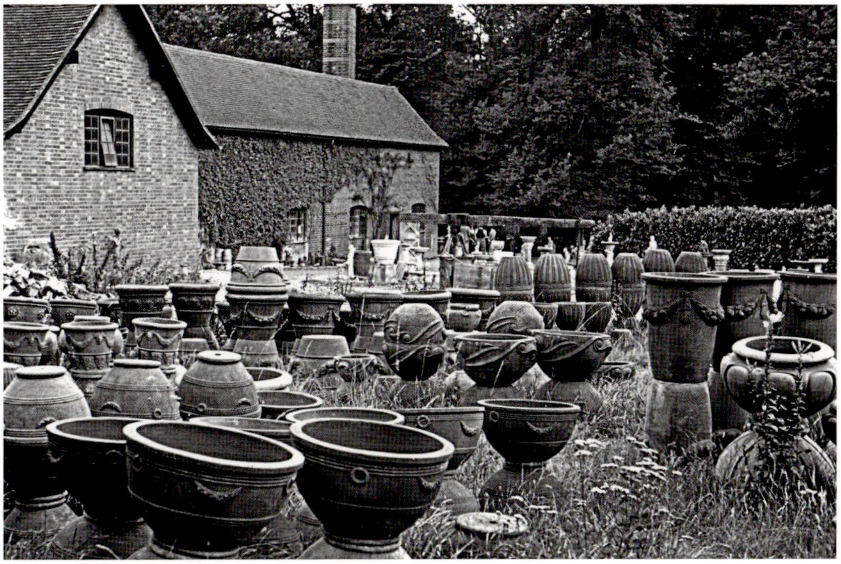

RIGHT
The Pottery stockyard, 1930s

The Watts Chapel itself, and the surrounding Watts Cemetery, form the most complete tribute to Mary's work as a designer and artistic collaborator. There are some sixty Compton Pottery terracotta gravestones in the Cemetery, giving the whole site a deeply satisfying coherence as an Arts & Crafts masterpiece in its own right.

In 1906 Mary added a decorative well-head at the Cemetery's northern boundary, and in 1911 completed the elegant brick Cloister that clings to the rising ground next to her husband's grave (Mary's ashes were interred alongside his in 1938). The Cloister was gradually filled with plaques commemorating local people, while at its mid-point, next to the low gates, is a memorial to GF Watts. Suitably Italianate for one known to his many friends as Signor, this was designed by Mary and incorporates relief interpretations of two of Watts's paintings and an effigy of the artist himself made by Thomas Wren who had come from Monkshatch to work as an assistant first to Watts and later to Mary. At the feet of the figure is a cherub holding a scroll on which appear the Latin words *Finis et Initium*: The End but also the Beginning.

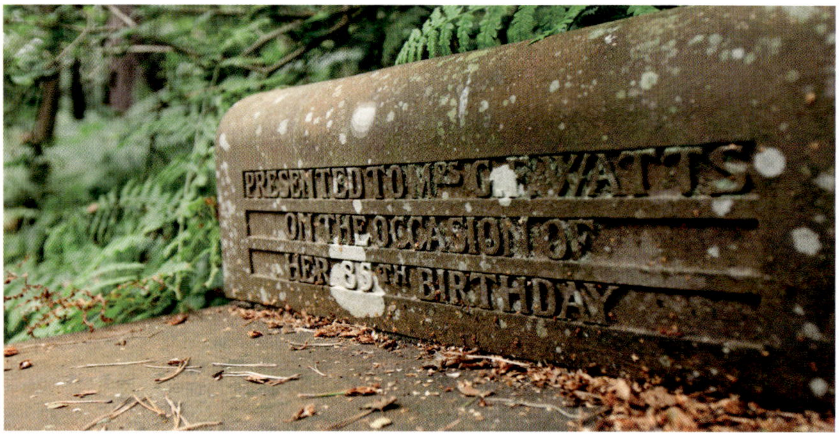

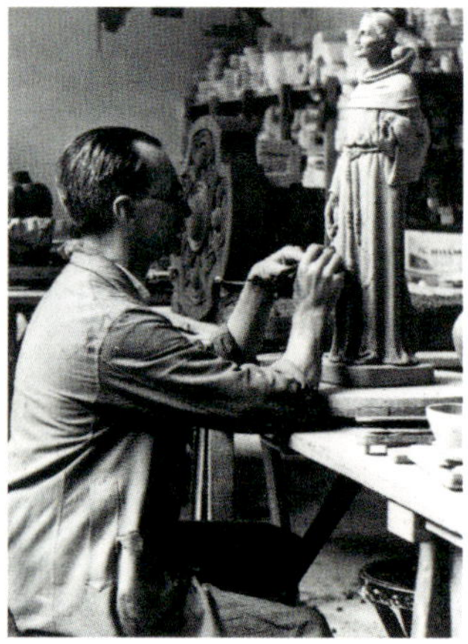

BELOW LEFT
Commemorative bench presented to Mary Watts on her 85th birthday, and installed in the grounds of Limnerslease

BELOW RIGHT
The modelling room of the Pottery with Thomas Wren working on a figurine

RIGHT
Lena Titcomb modelling a figure, 1930s

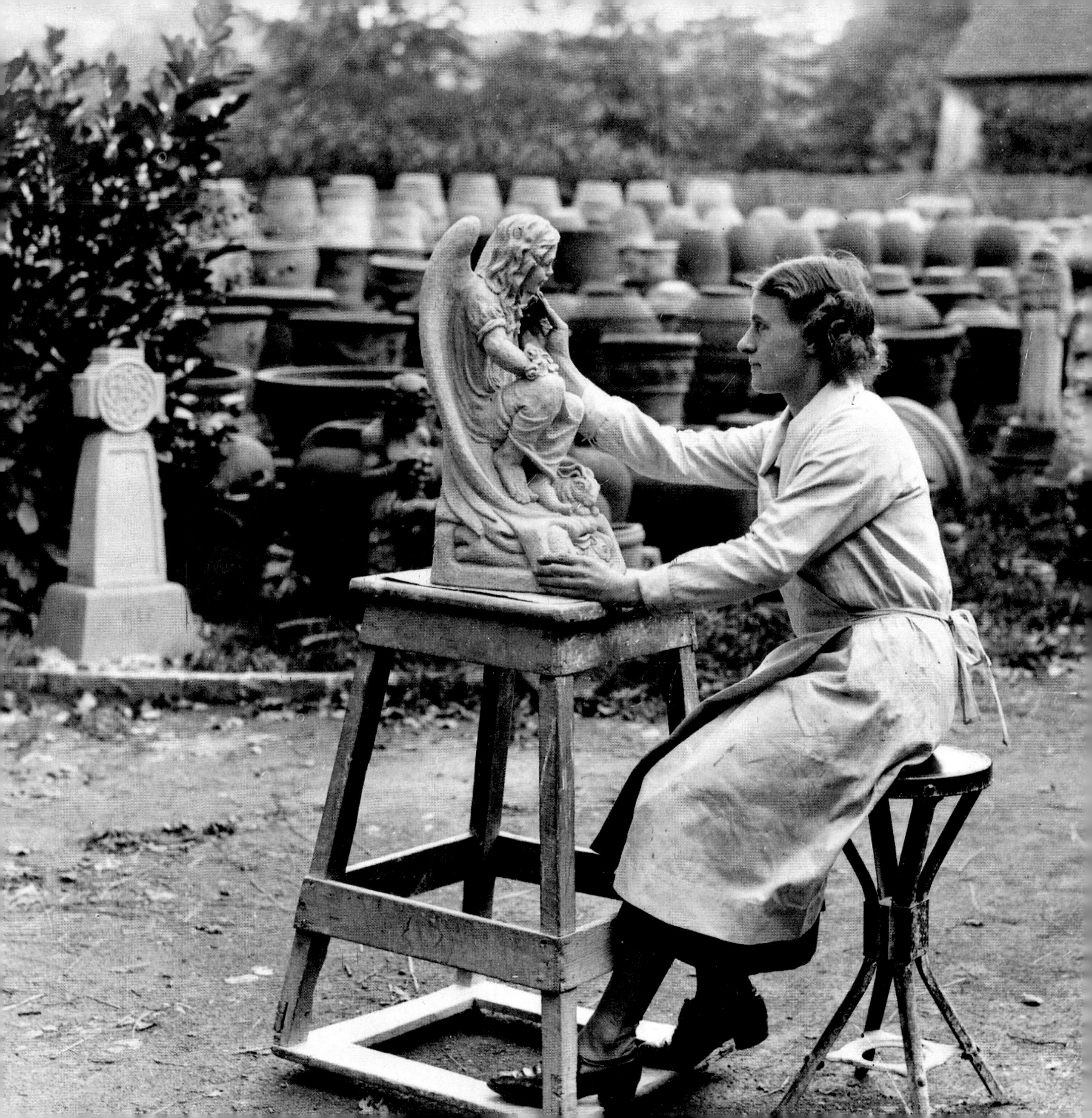

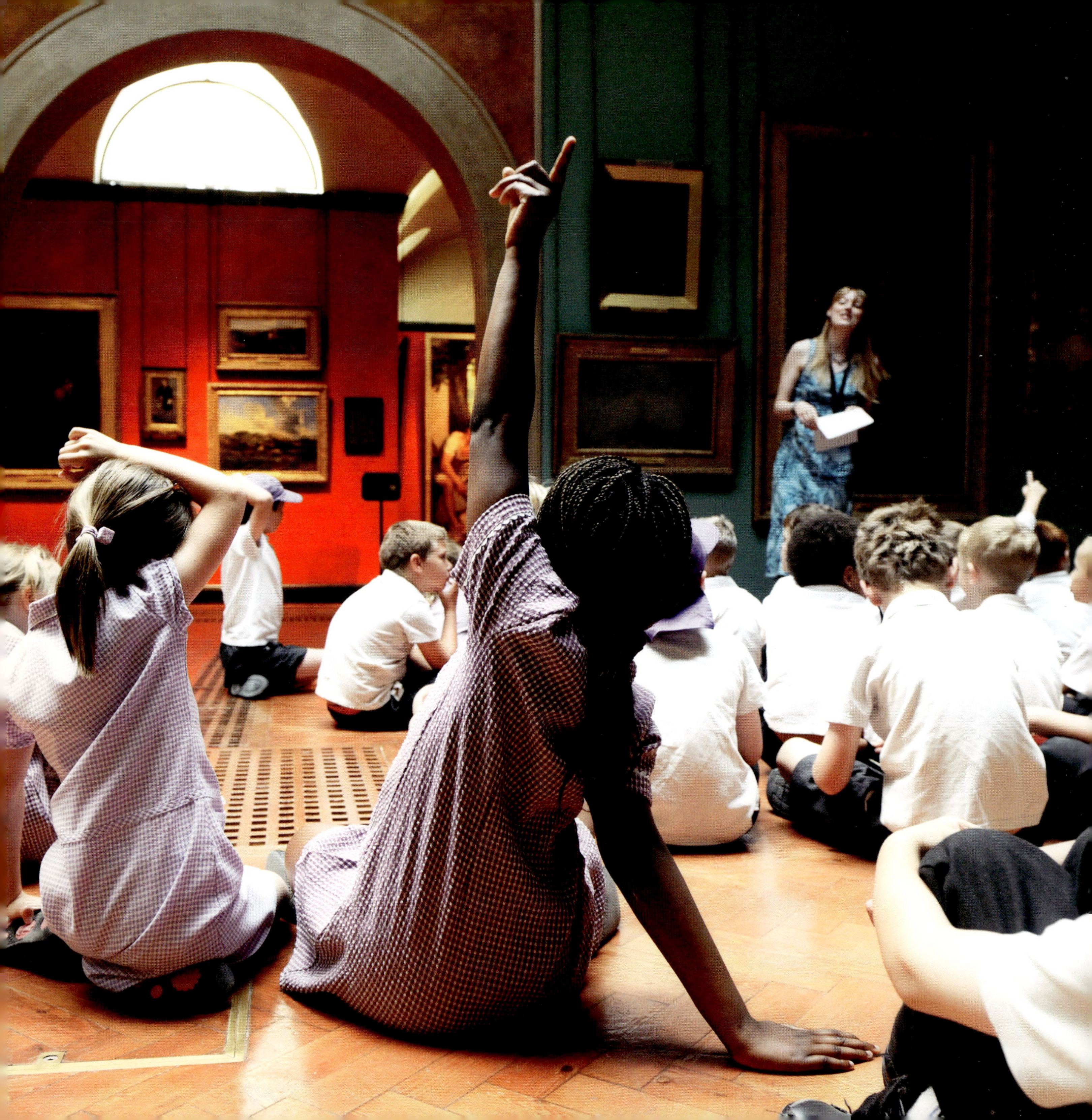

THE FOUNDING VISION OF GF WATTS AND MARY WATTS WAS TO DELIVER ART FOR ALL. THE GOAL OF ENHANCING AND TRANSFORMING PEOPLE'S LIVES THROUGH ART IS WHAT INSPIRES THE WORK AND ACTIVITIES TODAY AT WATTS GALLERY – ARTISTS' VILLAGE. WE ARE NOW BECOMING RECOGNISED AS THE LEADING CENTRE FOR EXPLORING VICTORIAN ART, SOCIAL HISTORY AND CRAFT – AND A BEACON FOR THE ARTS & CRAFTS. ABOVE ALL WE WILL CONTINUE TO SEEK TO OFFER ART FOR ALL.

LEFT
Children in the Isabel Goldsmith Patiño Gallery

ART FOR ALL

GF and Mary Watts have left us a vision: art, design and architecture created for the common good in collaboration with others of all abilities. As the Artists' Village they created is being revived, that vision remains central to all we do.

The Wattses had been brought together themselves by a shared vision of the social role of art and design – of the great potential of the visual arts to change people's lives for the better. Both had been early participants in the projects to bring art exhibitions and craft classes to London's East End, collaborations which evolved into the founding of the Whitechapel Art Gallery. The Wattses were advocates and supporters of many other progressive causes and organisations, from the campaign against restrictive clothing to the women's suffrage movement, from animal rights to the trade union movement. Never narrowly political in their outlook, they believed passionately in the progress of humanity and the role of art in that great process.

It was this determined optimism that carried Watts Gallery Trust through the challenging early years of the twenty-first century. One hundred years after the opening of the Watts Gallery in 1904, the building was dying. It was still beautiful, and deeply loved by those few who knew it, but it was at risk. The *Hope* campaign, aptly named after Watts's most famous painting, was launched in 2006 to restore the Gallery to its former glory. An appearance on the BBC's *Restoration Village* programme (we came second!) impressed the Gallery's existence on the minds of a new national public. But, along with a major grant awarded by the Heritage Lottery Fund, it was a grass-roots struggle to successfully fundraise to complete the restoration in 2011. And no sooner had the Gallery opened than a unique opportunity to acquire Limnerslease, the artists' home next door, presented itself. The Watts Studios at Limnerslease opened in 2016 but the restoration of the Watts Artists' Village continues. As ever, Watts Gallery Trust forges ahead without public subsidy. The Trust is dependent upon visitors, earned income (through the Tea Shop, Shop and Watts Contemporary exhibitions) and fundraising.

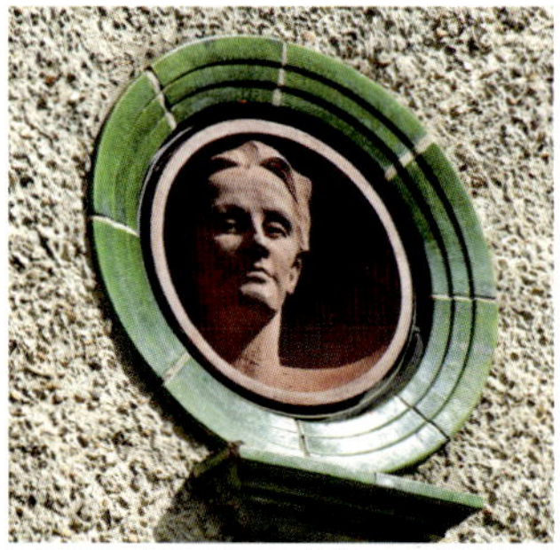

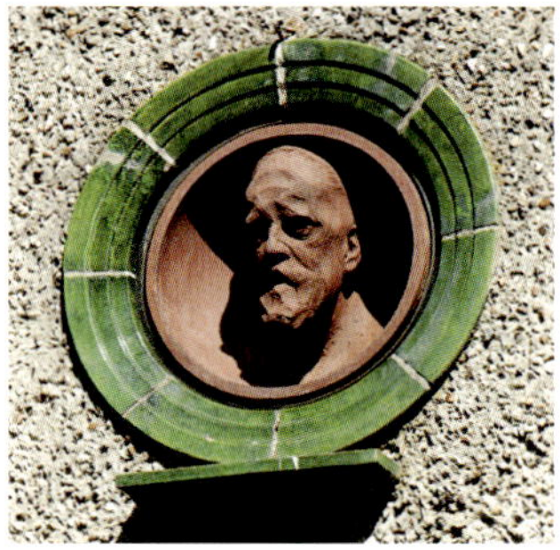

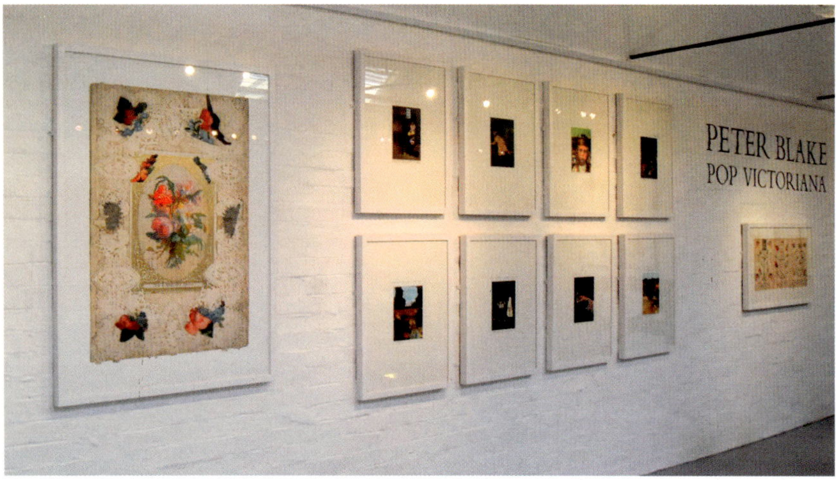

ABOVE (TOP)
Marcus Cornish, terracotta bust of Mary Watts, 2014

ABOVE (BOTTOM)
Marcus Cornish, terracotta bust of G F Watts, 2014

LEFT
Watts Contemporary exhibition

FAR RIGHT (TOP)
Watts Gallery entrance prior to the recent restoration

FAR RIGHT (BOTTOM)
Teracotta class at the Foyle Pottery Studio

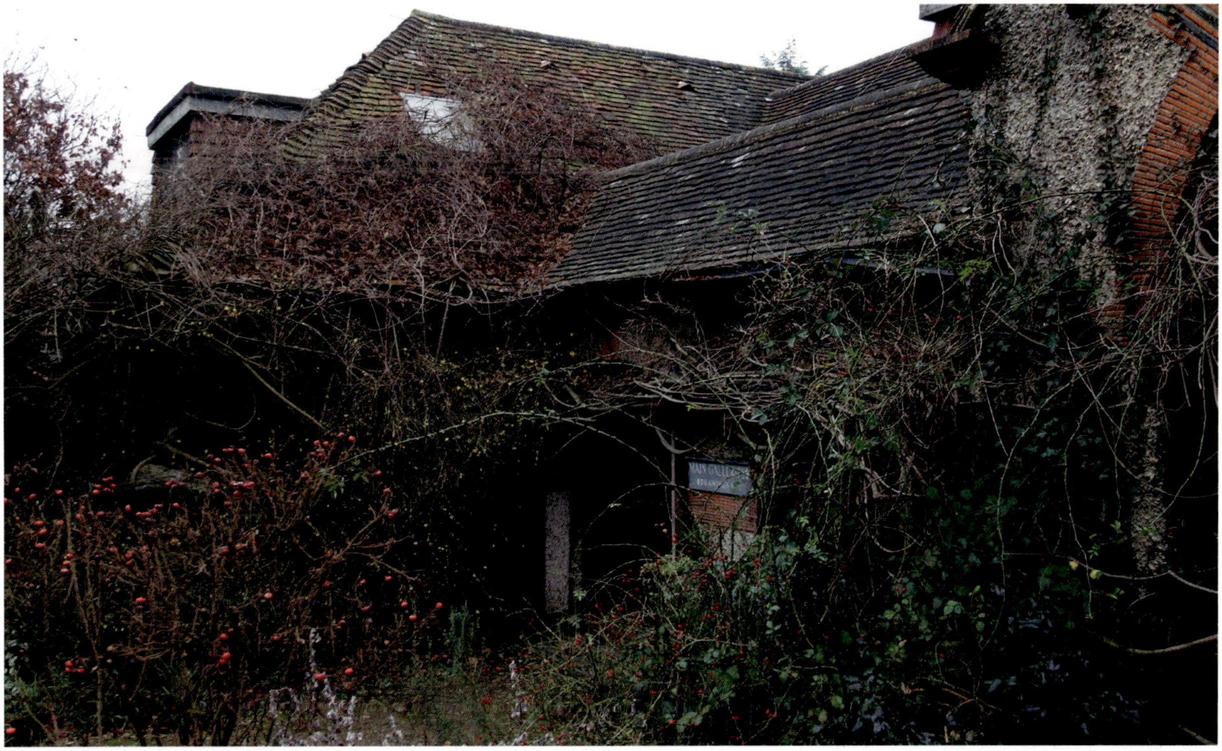

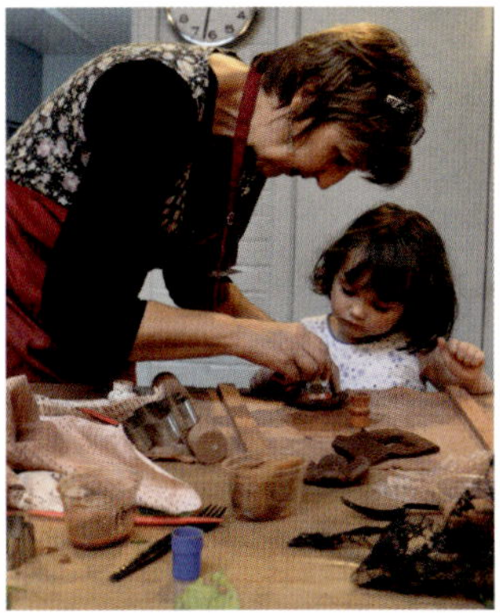

Watts Gallery Trust remains closely linked to its neighbours in Compton in many ways, not least in our management of the Watts Chapel and Cemetery, still living components of parish life. Our learning and engagement programmes reach out to many thousands of participants each year, who come to take classes in terracotta modelling (in the tradition of Mary Watts) and many other art media. We have a particular focus on bringing to the Gallery people who might otherwise risk exclusion from society on account of social deprivation or disability, and we collaborate with local prisons to bring the Watts vision even to those in custody.

At the centre of the Watts vision is collaboration, and we certainly have not travelled alone. Our staff are blessed to have the help and advice of two key bodies of people, our Trustees and our Volunteers, who all bring a wealth of experience and connections to the organisation. We collaborate internationally with comparable artists' estates abroad, for example Polenovo in rural Russia, whom we partnered to bring an exhibition of Russian Arts & Crafts to Compton in the winter of 2014–15. We partner universities too. We work with the City & Guilds of London Art School on conservation projects, notably in supporting the Conservation Studio at Limnerslease. The University for the Creative Arts in Farnham is our collaborator in the Watts Artist in Residence scheme and the Winsor and Newton Watts Painting Prize.

Today, the buildings where Mary Watts ran the Pottery house the Visitor Centre, Shop, the famous Watts Tea Shop, as well as the Watts Contemporary Gallery, a space for new art. Here you can purchase affordable modern art curated by the Gallery team. You can also enjoy the annual exhibitions of the work of our Artists in Residence. And a Watts Contemporary exhibition that always amazes is the Big Issues project. Working with prisoners, ex-offenders, young people at risk and other vulnerable people, our team start conversations and exchanges which lead to participants expressing their stories and concerns on paper or in clay and developing their voice and feelings through art. The resulting work is shown in the annual Big Issues exhibition – held in Compton and London – with the works offered for sale and all the proceeds returning to the artists. The scheme has literally saved lives by providing a second chance to those who have felt excluded or worthless. We truly offer Art for All.

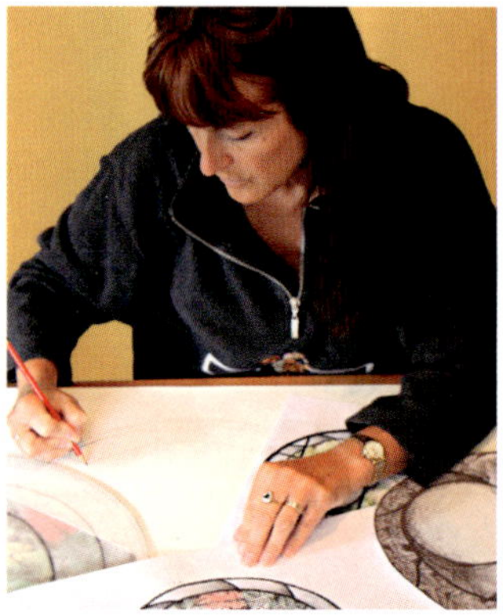

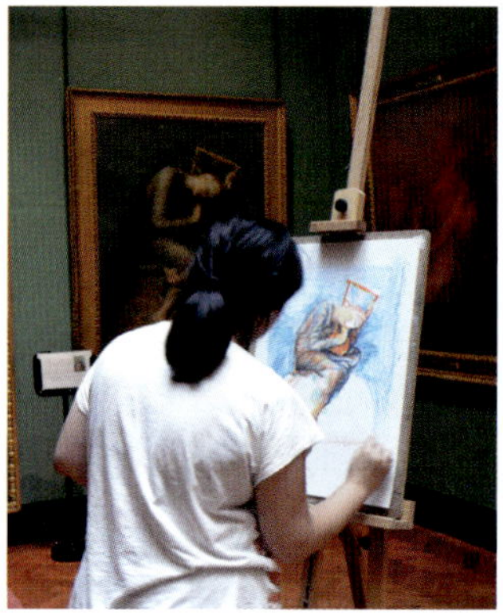

ABOVE (TOP)
Artist in Residence, Jennie Jewitt-Harris

ABOVE (BOTTOM)
A student drawing *Hope*
With kind permission of a private owner

RIGHT
Watts at Dusk evening event

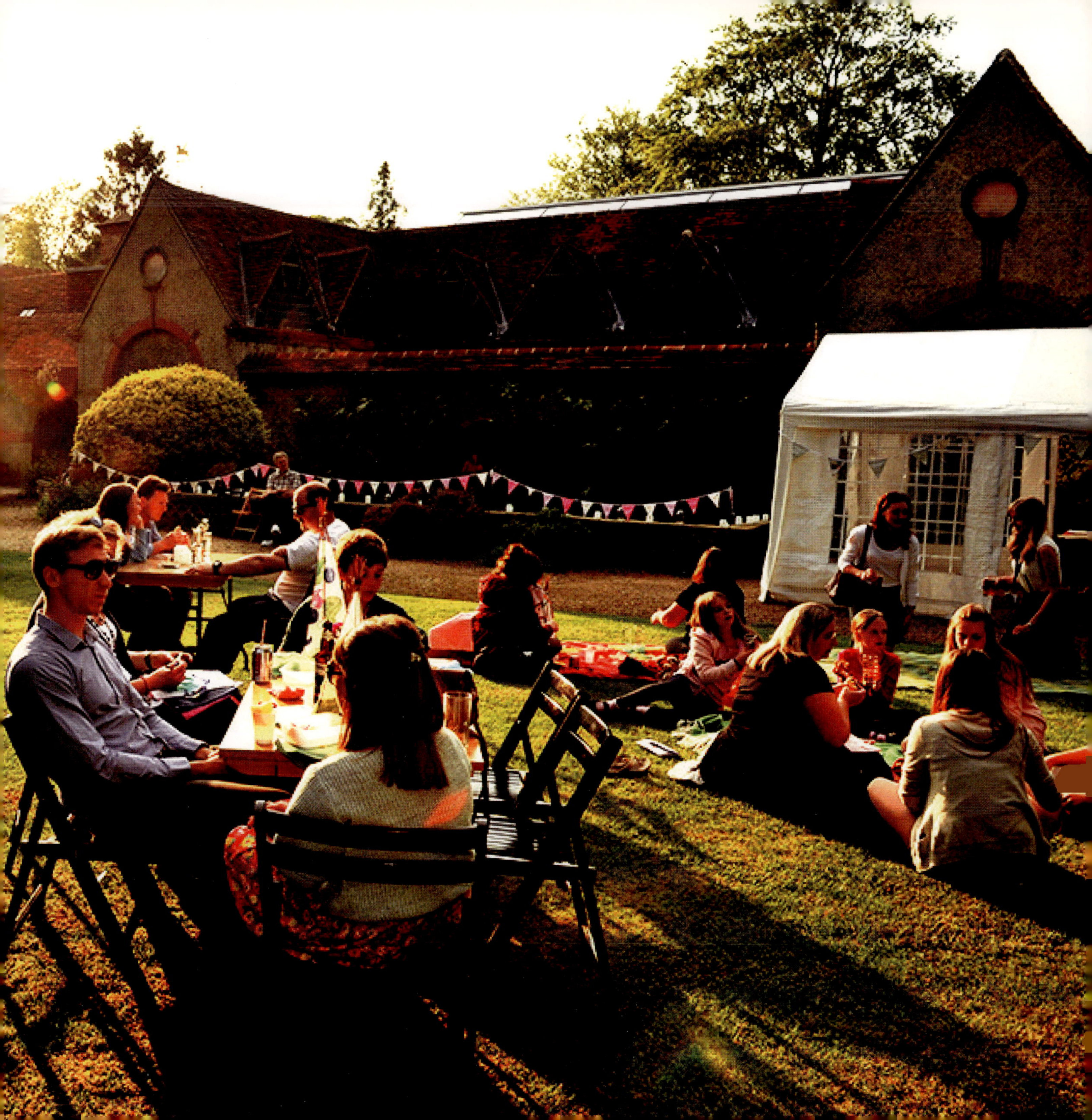

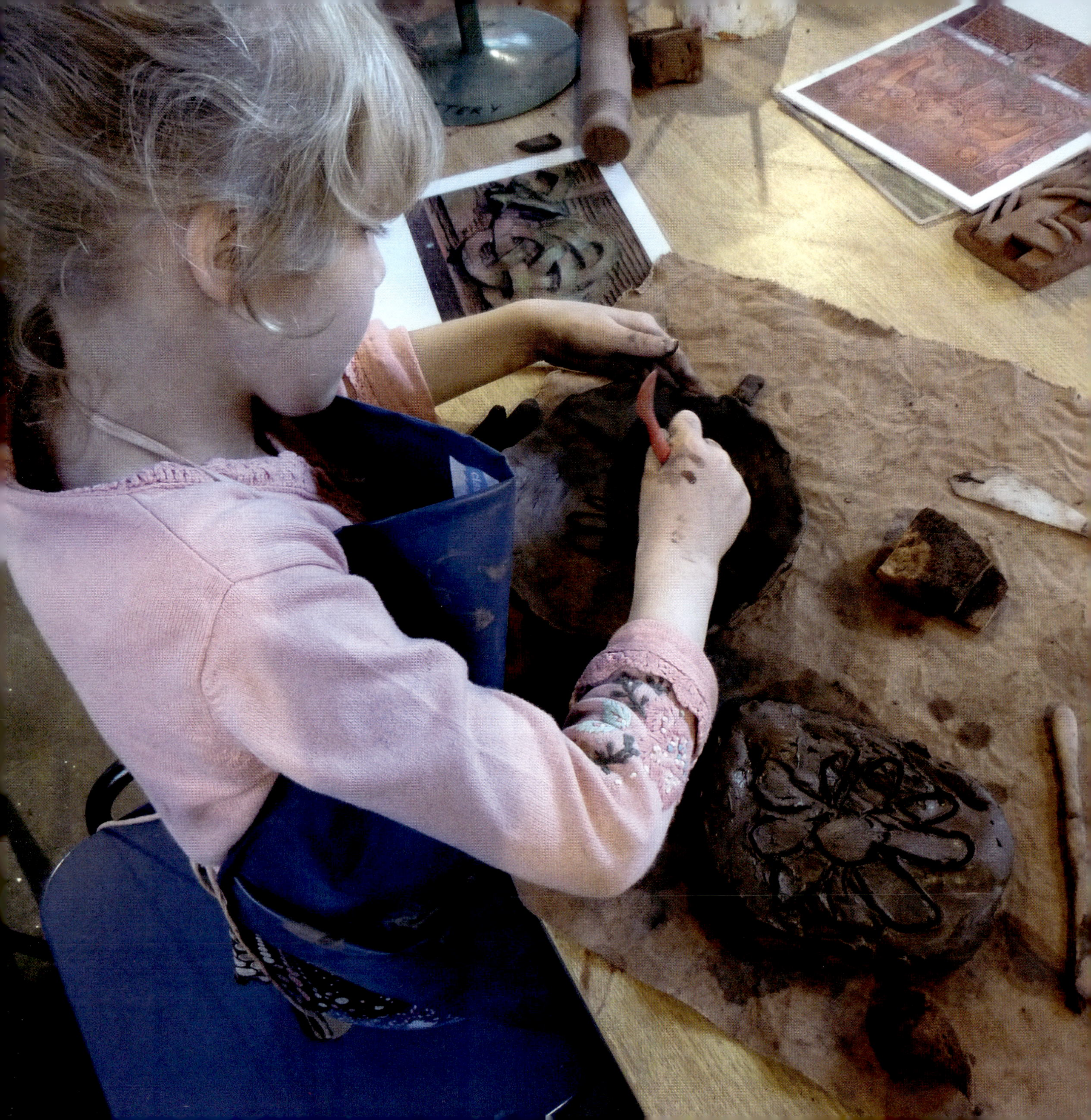

JOIN US!

Watts Gallery
Down Lane
Compton
Guildford
Surrey GU3 1DQ

Tel **01483 810235**
info@wattsgallery.org.uk

Please visit **www.wattsgallery.org.uk** to explore the many ways of getting to know Watts Gallery – Artists' Village.

Learning

We offer an inspiring year-round programme for adult learners, schools and universities, families, young people and community groups including weekly guided tours and art talks, lectures, film screenings, short courses, demonstrations, term-length practical evening classes, evening events, family drop-in activities, artist- and actor-led workshops for schools as well as Arts Award accredited programmes for young people.
www.wattsgallery.org.uk/learn

Book a Tour of Limnerslease

The parts of Limnerslease not normally open to the public are still accessible through guided tours. To book, please contact us on **01483 813593**, **info@wattsgallery.org.uk**, **www.wattsgallery.org.uk/artists-village/limnerslease**

Volunteer

Watts Gallery – Artists' Village depends on its volunteers who receive regular training. It's enjoyable, sociable, rewarding and valuable work. Contact us if you would like to know more.
www.wattsgallery.org.uk/join-us/volunteering

Become a Friend

If you would like to enjoy free admission, get involved in exclusive events and talks and be the first to view new exhibitions, then becoming a Friend of Watts Gallery – Artists' Village is for you.
www.wattsgallery.org.uk/join-us/friend

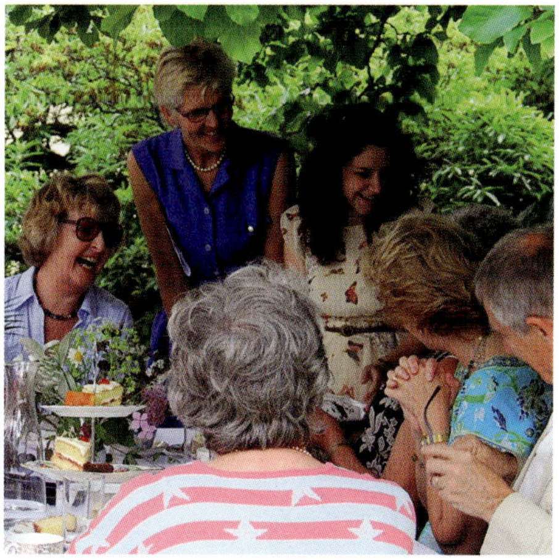

READING AND RESEARCH

THERE ARE NOW SEVERAL EXCELLENT BOOKS ABOUT THE WATTSES AND WATTS GALLERY – ARTISTS' VILLAGE:

Watts Gallery – Artists' Village

Mark Bills, ed., *An Artists' Village. GF Watts and Mary Watts at Compton* (Watts Gallery 2011)

Mary Watts, *The Word in the Pattern. A Key to the Symbols on the Walls of the Chapel at Compton* (Ward 1905) [reprinted in 2012 by the Society for the Arts and Crafts Movement in Surrey, with new introductory essays]

Mark Bills, *Watts Chapel. A Guide to the Symbols of Mary Watts's Arts and Crafts Masterpiece* (Philip Wilson 2010)

Hilary Grainger, *The Architecture of Sir Ernest George* (Spire 2011)

Fiona Curtis, *Guide to Compton Village* (forthcoming 2016)

GF Watts

Mary Watts, *George Frederic Watts: The Annals of an Artist's Life*, 3 vols (Macmillan 1912) [available free online at **www.archive.org**]

Wilfrid Blunt, *'England's Michelangelo': A Biography of George Frederic Watts* (Hamish Hamilton 1975)

Veronica Franklin Gould, *GF Watts: The Last Great Victorian* (Yale University Press 2004)

Barbara Bryant, *GF Watts Portraits. Fame and Beauty in Victorian Society* (National Portrait Gallery 2004)

Mark Bills and Barbara Bryant, *Victorian Visionary. Highlights from the Watts Gallery Collection* (Yale University Press 2008)

Mary Watts

Veronica Franklin Gould, *Mary Seton Watts (1849–1938): Unsung Heroine of the Art Nouveau* (Watts Gallery 1998)

Mary McMahon, *The Making of Mary Seton Watts* (Watts Gallery 2013)

If you are interested in doing further research about the Wattses, the two major holdings of manuscripts are:

National Portrait Gallery Archive

www.npg.org.uk/research/archive/collected-archives/the-watts-collection.php

Watts Gallery Archive

www.wattsgallery.org.uk/artists-village/watts-library-archive/

BIRDS

Watts Gallery – Artists' Village lies close to the North Downs, right alongside the Pilgrims' Way, and has a rich variety of bird habitats including mature mixed woodland and hedgerows. Species such as **great spotted woodpeckers**, **nuthatches**, **treecreepers**, **great** and **coal tits**, **goldcrests** and **jays** can be seen virtually all year round, and one of the most beautiful British birds, the **bullfinch**, is also a regular visitor and breeds locally. **Owls**, both tawny and little, are also present, but are more likely to be heard than seen with clear autumn nights the best possibility. In winter the area around the gallery also attracts migrant **thrushes** from Continental Europe, particularly **fieldfares**.

In spring and summer the Artists' Village is an excellent place to hear the dawn chorus which lasts right up to the end of June with the best time being between six and eight o'clock in the morning. The very rare **firecrest**, the smallest British bird, can also be found occasionally in the woods nearby.

Illustrations by Donna Scott

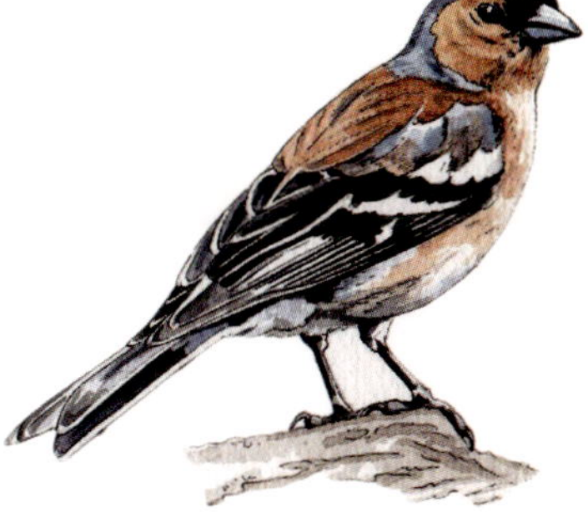

CHAFFINCH

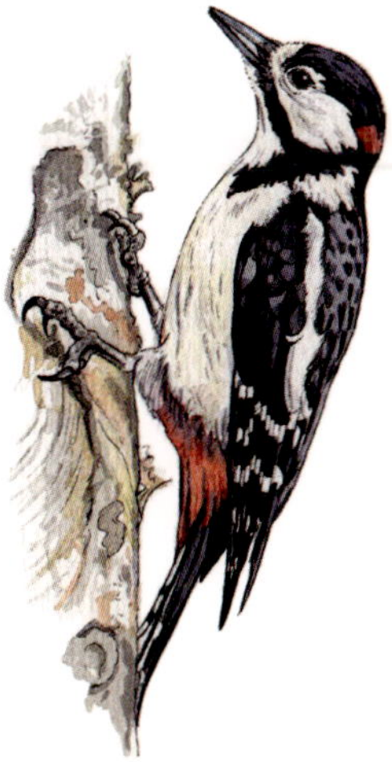

GREAT SPOTTED WOODPECKER

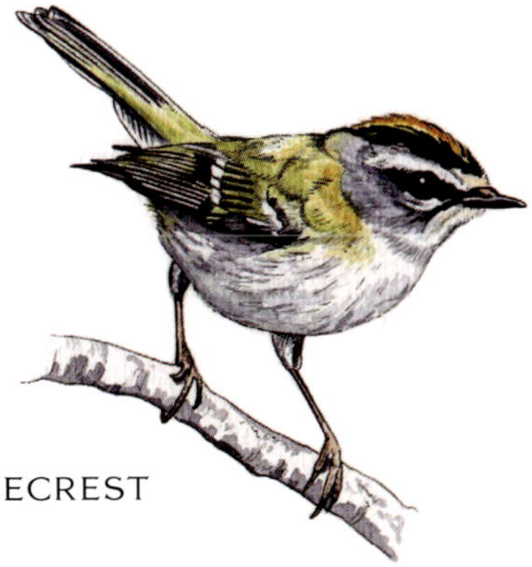

FIRECREST

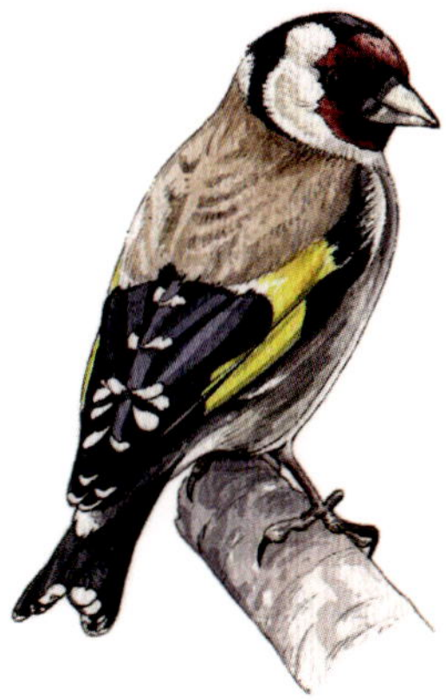

GOLDFINCH

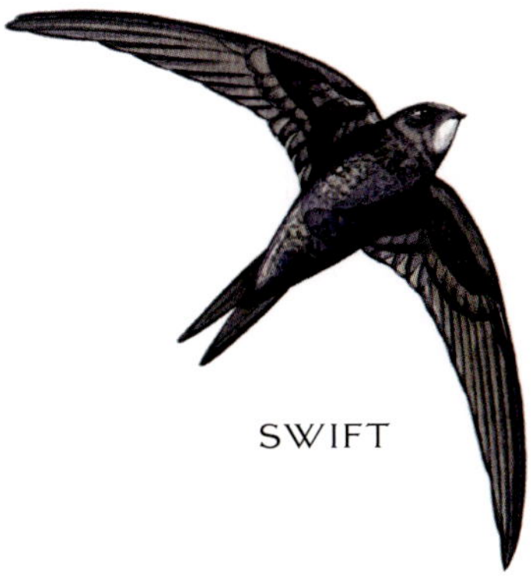

SWIFT

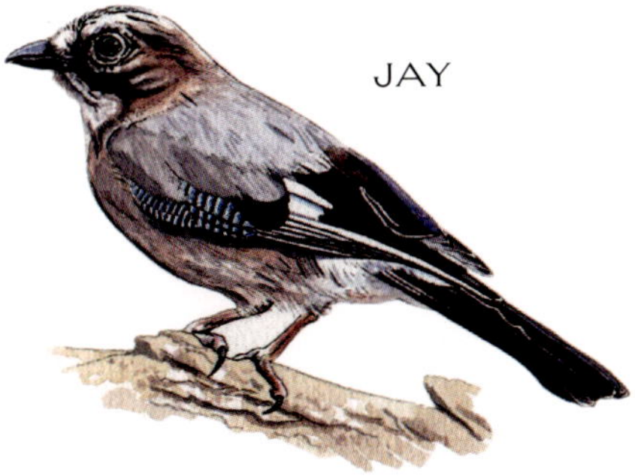

JAY

COMPTON VILLAGE CIRCULAR WALK

FROM WATTS GALLERY – ARTISTS' VILLAGE
APPROXIMATELY TWO AND A QUARTER MILES

Opposite the main Gallery entrance on Down Lane, notice the terracotta drinking fountain installed for the use of walkers by Mary Watts in the wall of **Brixbury**, formerly the Wattses' coach house. Turn left along Down Lane towards **Watts Chapel and Cemetery**. Continue in the same direction to the end of Down Lane and turn left onto The Street. Opposite you will see **Little Cottage**, where the 1901 census reveals that James Nicol, pottery manager, first lodged. Next door but one is **Moors Cottage**, the origins of which go back to the early part of the 17th century. When the Wattses lived in Compton the cottage was a coffee house and the manager expressed pride in having served tea and coffee to clientele from all continents, as the reputation of Watts Gallery spread far and wide.

Continue until you reach a small antiques shop, opposite which you will see the **Compton War Memorial**, which was designed by Mary Watts and unveiled in 1922. The Grade I listed **St Nicholas' Church**, with origins that date from the 10th/11th century, is just a short walk from here and well worth a visit. The double chancel makes a particularly interesting feature, as do the opening to what was an anchorite's cell and the Norman marking next to the pulpit that is thought to have been scratched into the stone by a crusader praying for a safe return.

On leaving the Church, continue in the same direction: **White Hart Cottage** is immediately visible. The cottage originates from the early 16th century and was once a Public House. Opposite the entrance to Puck's Oak Barn is the **Old Forge**. This was once the home of Clarence Sex the blacksmith. Clarence produced the ornate ironwork that forms part of the Watts Chapel doors and the gates to the Watts Cemetery Cloister.

A little further along the road you will see **Compton Village Hall**, built in 1934 following a local fundraising effort which raised £2,982, a proportion of which was donated by Mary Watts who laid the foundation stone. Continue, passing the Green and the Common to your left, then turn left into Withies Lane. Before reaching the 16th-century public house, **The Withies Inn**, you will see four Arts & Crafts-style cottages, **One to Four Oak Cottages**. Ernest George (the architect of Limnerslease) built these at Mary's request for members of her Potters' Guild. Numbers five and six are thought to have been designed by Clough Williams-Ellis, architect of the village of Portmeirion in North Wales. The Compton potter George Aubertin lived at number five until his death in 1970 and former pottery manager James Nicol also resided here.

Continue up Withies Lane, passing the public house and turn right onto Polsted lane where you pass Polsted Manor (now apartments). Pass the turning to the left and continue on to the next turning which is the **Pilgrims' Way**. Turn left and this will take you back to Watts Gallery – Artists' Village where you will find the Tea Shop for a well-deserved rest and bite to eat.

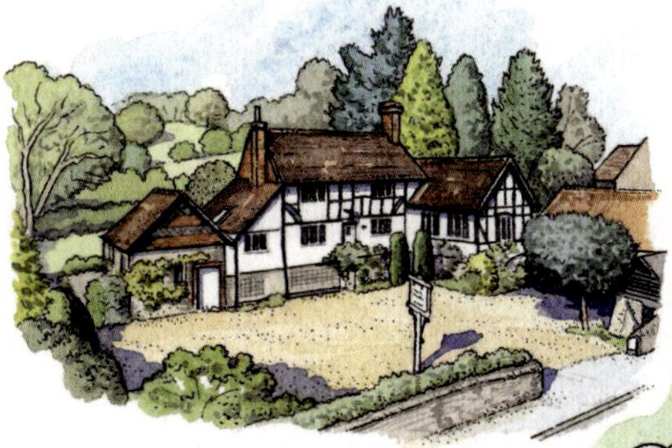

MOORS COTTAGE

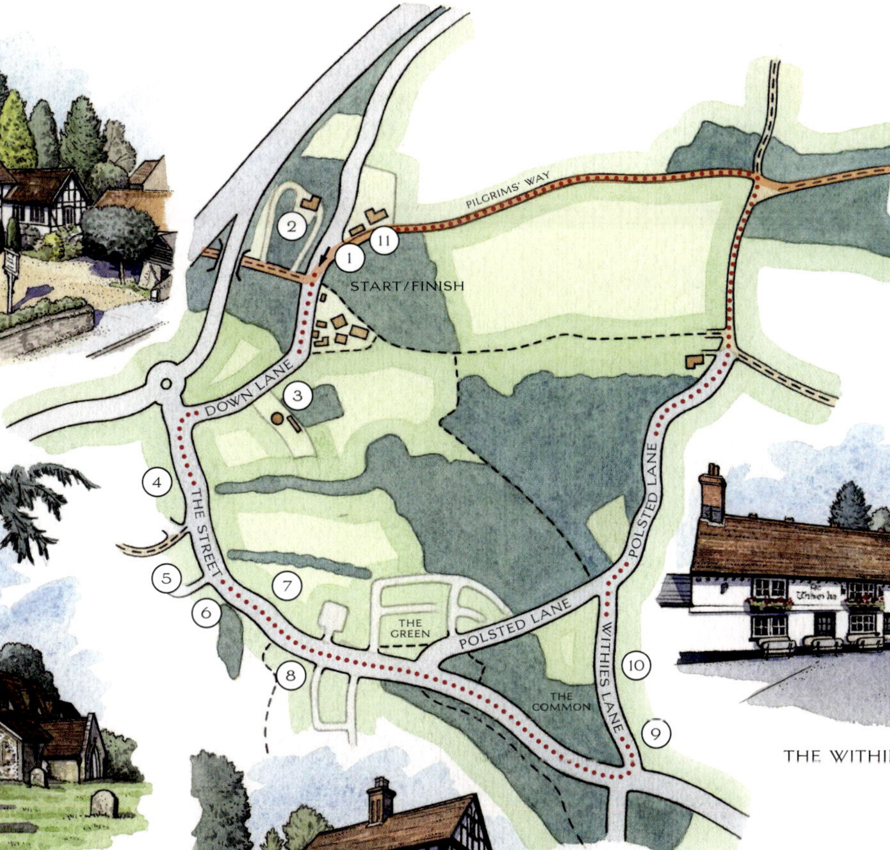

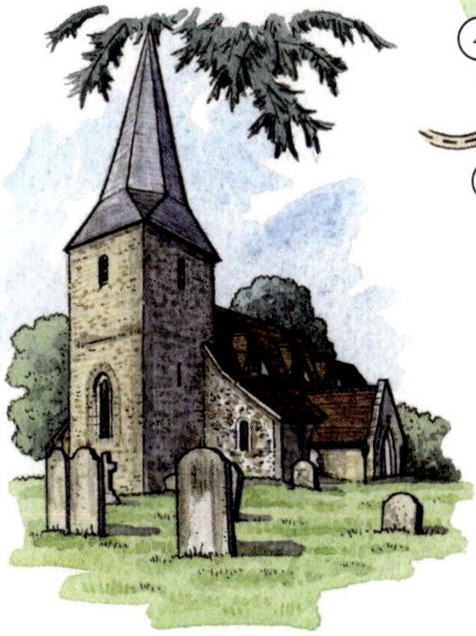

ST NICHOLAS' CHURCH

"SURREY'S FLAGSHIP NORMAN CHURCH"

England's Thousand Best Churches,
Simon Jenkins

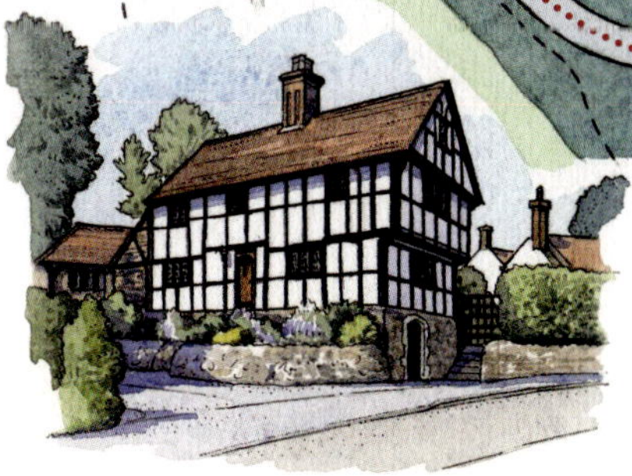

WHITE HART COTTAGE

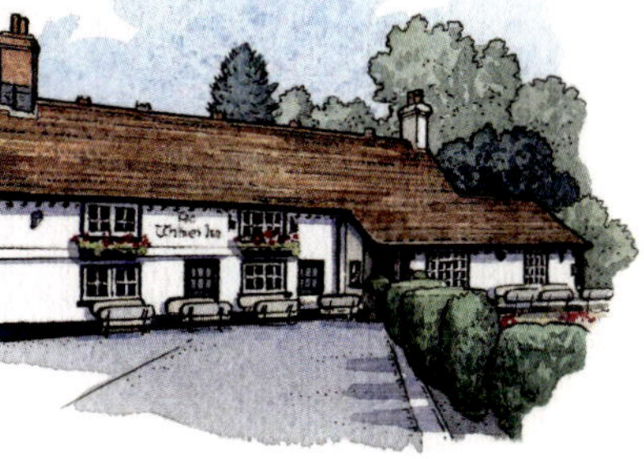

THE WITHIES INN

Illustration by Donna Scott

- COMPTON VILLAGE WALK ROUTE (red dotted line)
- PILGRIMS' WAY (orange line)
- OTHER PUBLIC RIGHTS OF WAY (dashed line)

1. START – WATTS GALLERY – ARTISTS' VILLAGE
2. LIMNERSLEASE
3. WATTS CHAPEL & CEMETERY
4. MOORS COTTAGE
5. ST NICHOLAS CHURCH & WAR MEMORIAL
6. WHITE HART COTTAGE
7. THE OLD FORGE
8. COMPTON VILLAGE HALL
9. OAK COTTAGES
10. THE WITHIES INN
11. FINISH – THE TEA SHOP AT WATTS GALLERY – ARTISTS' VILLAGE

OTHER PLACES TO VISIT

THERE ARE MANY OTHER INTERESTING PLACES, OPEN TO THE PUBLIC, WHERE YOU CAN LEARN MORE ABOUT THE LIFE AND WORK OF GF WATTS. MANY MUSEUMS AND GALLERIES AROUND THE UK HOLD EXAMPLES OF HIS WORK, BUT HERE ARE SOME HIGHLIGHTS:

Tate Britain

The Tate collection of works by GF Watts is second only to that of Watts Gallery itself. Only a small proportion of the collection is however on show at any one time.
www.tate.org.uk/visit/tate-britain

National Portrait Gallery

Watts donated some of his greatest portraits to the NPG to create what was known as the Hall of Fame. Many of these portraits are on show both in London and at the NPG's outpost in North Wales.
www.npg.org.uk/beyond/bodelwyddan-castle.php

The Watts Memorial to Heroic Self-Sacrifice

An extraordinary little building in the City of London in what is known as Postman's Park. The Memorial, designed by Watts, was opened in 1900 to commemorate ordinary people who had laid down their lives to save others.
www.postmanspark.org.uk

St Paul's Cathedral

The mosaics in the spandrels under the Whispering Gallery representing the four Evangelists are based on designs made by Watts.
www.stpauls.co.uk

Church of St James the Less

A lovely and lively Victorian church near Tate Britain in Pimlico, London. Watts created the chancel arch image of Christ and the Evangelists.
www.sjtl.org

Church of St Giles-in-the-Fields

Inside this London church is the mosaic version of Watts's famous image of *Time, Death and Judgement* that was originally placed on the street front of St Jude's in Whitechapel.
www.stgilesonline.org

Leighton House Museum

The former home and studio of Watts's great friend, the painter Frederic Leighton, in Kensington. The garden of Watts's own London house, now demolished, adjoined this beautiful residence. The collection includes Watts's portrait of Leighton.
www.rbkc.gov.uk/subsites/museums/leightonhousemuseum/visitus.aspx

7 Hammersmith Terrace

The London home of the great printer Emery Walker who collaborated with Mary Watts to make colour reproductions of paintings by GF Watts which carried his imagery across the world.
www.emerywalker.org.uk

Eastnor Castle

This romantic castle near Ledbury in Herefordshire was the seat of Lord and Lady Somers, close friends of Watts. The collection includes a group of his finest portraits.
www.eastnorcastle.com

Details of our international network of artists' studio museums can be found on this website
www.studiomuseumnetwork.org